W9-BIN-878

TerraNova

Reading/Language Arts Coach
Grade 8

TerraNova Reading/Language Arts Coach, Grade 8
EDI 152
ISBN: 1-58620-080-1

Editor: Norma Brenes
Interior Design: Lauren Kampel
Cover Design: Andrea Raiola

Educational Design
345 Hudson Street, New York, NY 10014-4502
Copyright © 2002 Educational Design, an imprint of Triumph Learning.
A division of Haights Cross Communications.
All rights reserved. No part of this publication may be reproduced in whole or in part, stored in a retrieval system, or transmitted in any form or by any means, electronic, mechanical, photocopying, recording or otherwise, without written permission from the publisher.
Printed in the United States of America

Credits
Cover: © Chip Henderson/Index Stock
        Gateway Arch
        St. Louis, Missouri

TABLE OF CONTENTS

NOTICE: Photocopying any part of this book is forbidden by law.

NOTICE: Photocopying any part of this book is forbidden by law.

NOTICE: Photocopying any part of this book is forbidden by law.

TO THE STUDENT

This book can help you become a better reader, writer, and thinker. It will help you do well on both the Reading and the Language Arts parts of the **TerraNova Test**.

Every day, you use the reading and writing skills reviewed in this book. But here's the difference: the examples, practice selections, and tips in this book can help you use them better.

Here's how:

✔ They can help you think about and understand what test questions are really asking you to do.

✔ They can help you feel more confident with answer choices.

✔ They can help you write better answers in your own words.

Have fun while you practice. We hope you like the stories.

NOTICE: Photocopying any part of this book is forbidden by law.

7

PART 1: READING AND ANSWERING MULTIPLE-CHOICE QUESTIONS

NOTICE: Photocopying any part of this book is forbidden by law.

9

1 HOW TO READ AND ANSWER MULTIPLE-CHOICE QUESTIONS

GETTING THE IDEA

Most tests ask you to read a passage and answer some questions. Those questions are often multiple-choice. Multiple-choice questions can look like the following:

1 In the writer's opinion, who was the greatest baseball player?

   A   Ty Cobb

   B   Babe Ruth

   C   Hank Aaron

   D   Mickey Mantle

2 This passage is mainly about

   A   the President of the United States

   B   how a bill is passed in Congress

   C   how a bill gets to Congress

   D   what a Congressperson does

Notice that each question has a number in front of it. Each answer choice has a letter in front of it. Only one answer choice is correct.

Use these tips when you are answering a multiple-choice question:

1. **Read the entire question and its answer choices first**.

2. **Find key words in the question and underline them**. Key words let you know exactly what is being asked. Key words include:

   • the question words *who*, *what*, *when*, *where*, *why*, *which*, and *how*

   • words that tell time order, such as *first*, *next*, *before*, and *after*

   • words that signal why something happens, such as *because*, *effect*, *cause*, and *result*.

   • words that give information, such as *not*, *best*, *most*, *mainly*, *opposite*, and *same as*

 NOTICE: Photocopying any part of this book is forbidden by law.

Read the following multiple-choice questions. Look for key words. They are underlined in each example.

Who is the main character in this story?

Which word means the same as *reliable*?

Which of these shows the best way to combine these sentences?

Based on the clues in the passage, he is probably

Which of the following is not an example of serendipity?

What most likely will happen next?

This passage is mostly about

3. **Read the passage.**

4. **Reread the question and all the answer choices.** Eliminate answer choices you know are incorrect. Then select the best answer from the remaining choices. Before marking your answer, skim the passage for stated information or for clues.

5. **Mark your answer carefully.** Double-check your answer.

Read the example below. Use what you have learned to answer the question.

Example 1

The Nile is the world's longest river. It flows northward from its source in the snow-covered mountains of East Africa. It passes through the countries of Uganda, Ethiopia, Sudan, and Egypt. As it flows northward it carries silt, a mixture of soil and rocks. Finally, the Nile empties into the Mediterranean Sea.

1 **Where is the source of the Nile River?**

    A   in the Mediterranean Sea

    B   in Egypt

    C   in South Africa

    D   in the mountains of East Africa

NOTICE: Photocopying any part of this book is forbidden by law.

From reading the question, you learn that the passage is about the Nile River. The key words are *where*, *source*, and *Nile River*. The correct answer will tell you the source of the Nile River.

After reading the passage and rereading the question and answer choices, you can do the following to help you know the correct answer.

Cross out the answer choices that you know are wrong.

Choice A is wrong because the passage says that the Nile empties into the Mediterranean Sea. Choice C is incorrect because South Africa is not even mentioned in the passage.

Check back in the passage to find the information.

The second sentence in the passage says that the Nile flows from its source in the snow-covered mountains of East Africa. So you know that Choice **D** is the correct answer.

Now try this example. As you will see, sometimes the answer to the question is not directly stated in the passage. However, you can use clues in the passage to determine the correct answer choice.

Example 2

Ms. Sanders got up from her desk and walked to the window. She looked out at the schoolyard, where the graduating class was lining up with their teachers. They were practicing for tomorrow evening's graduation. Ms. Sanders was especially proud of this class. She thought back to the day she had welcomed them to Ashford Middle School.

2 **Who is Ms. Sanders?**

    A   a parent

    B   an eighth grader

    C   the school secretary

    D   the school principal

The key words are *who* and *Ms. Sanders*. Did you underline them?

NOTICE: Photocopying any part of this book is forbidden by law.

The passage says nothing about a parent or the school secretary. You can cross out Choices A and C. It is also likely that since the title "Ms. Sanders" is used, the person is an adult, not an eighth grader. Clues in some sentences tell you that Ms. Sanders was proud of the graduates, and she had welcomed them to the school. Since this is something the principal is likely to do, you can figure out that Ms. Sanders is the school principal. The correct answer is Choice **D**.

Do Example 3. Use the steps you have learned.

Example 3

      Kate was feeling down as she walked through the mall. Only that morning, her best friend Roxanne had announced she was moving to San Francisco. Kate knew she would really miss Roxanne, and she wanted to do something special for her. Just then she passed the jewelry store she and Roxanne had browsed in only last week. Kate remembered the beautiful turquoise earrings Roxanne had admired. Were they still there?

3   **What will Kate probably do next?**

    A   She will move to San Francisco, too.

    B   She will call Roxanne and tell her to come to the mall.

    C   She will buy the earrings as a gift for Roxanne.

    D   She will decide not to speak to Roxanne any more.

Did you underline the key words *Kate*, *probably*, and *do next*?

The correct answer is Choice **C**. You can eliminate choices A and D right away. It isn't likely that Kate will be able to move, too. It also doesn't make sense for her not to talk to her friend just because she is moving. Choice B is possible, since Kate and Roxanne have shopped at the mall together before. But the passage says Kate wants to do something special for her friend. She remembers the earrings her friend liked, so Choice **C** is the best answer.

NOTICE: Photocopying any part of this book is forbidden by law.

TIPS AND STRATEGIES
FOR READING AND
ANSWERING MULTIPLE-CHOICE QUESTIONS

☛ Read the question and answer choices first.

☛ Find and underline **key words** in the question. Remember that key words will point you to the kind of information the question is asking for. Kinds of key words include:

- question words such as *who, what, when, where, why, which,* and *how*

- words that signal time order, such as *first, next, then, before, after,* and *finally*

- words such as *not, best, most, mainly, opposite,* and *same as*

☛ After reading a passage, reread the question and answer choices. Cross out answer choices that you know right away are wrong. Then check back in a passage to locate specific information that will help you choose the correct answer.

☛ Mark your answer choice carefully. If you fill in the wrong answer by mistake, be sure to erase the mark completely. Then mark the right answer.

☛ Double-check your answer.

☛ If a long passage has two or more multiple-choice questions, read all of the questions and answer choices first. Find and underline the key words in each question. Then read the passage.

NOTICE: Photocopying any part of this book is forbidden by law.

SELECTIONS FOR PRACTICE

Selection 1

The Inca Empire rose out of a small village called Cuzco in a fertile valley in the Andes Mountains of Peru. The Inca settled in Cuzco about 1200 CE, to grow maize and other crops. Originally, the word *Inca* was the name for the ruler, but later the word was applied to all the people.

1 **What did the word *Inca* mean at first?**

    A   a type of crop

    B   the ruler

    C   the empire

    D   all the people

Selection 2

Mount St. Helens, in the Cascade Range of Washington State, was built by many eruptions over the years. At the beginning of 1980, it was 9, 677 feet high. People knew it was a volcano, but it had not erupted since 1857. Then on May 18, 1980, Mount St. Helens literally blew its top. The next day, the mountain was about 1,300 feet shorter than it had been the morning before. Today it measures 8, 363 feet.

2 **How high is Mount St. Helens now?**

    A   1,300 feet

    B   1,857 feet

    C   8, 363 feet

    D   9, 677 feet

NOTICE: Photocopying any part of this book is forbidden by law.

Selection 3

A deodorant destroys bad smells. People use deodorants for personal care as well as to remove odors in homes, work places, and cars.

Cats use deodorants, too. They spend hours licking their fur. Their saliva has a natural deodorant. For this reason, cats don't have an odor. This is not true of dogs, however. Everyone reminds me to spray deodorant in my car after my dog has ridden in it.

3   **According to this passage, which statement is true?**

    A   Cats often have an odor that some people dislike.

    B   Dogs have a natural deodorant.

    C   Almost all animals have a natural deodorant.

    D   Dogs have an odor that some people dislike.

Selection 4

The park was green and shady and there were plenty of benches. Anna chose a bench near the pond where she could watch the ducks. She sat down and opened the bag she had brought with her. She took out her sandwich and a bottle of iced tea.

After Anna ate her lunch, she glanced at her watch. She still had twenty minutes, so she spent the time listening to the quacking sounds of the ducks and enjoying the warm spring sunshine.

"I'm glad I decided to bring my lunch today," she thought to herself. "This is so much nicer than eating in the cafeteria."

4   **Anna feels that eating her lunch in the park is**

    A   not as good as eating in the cafeteria

    B   too expensive

    C   cheaper than buying lunch in the cafeteria

    D   pleasant and relaxing

NOTICE: Photocopying any part of this book is forbidden by law.

PART 2:
BASIC UNDERSTANDING

NOTICE: Photocopying any part of this book is forbidden by law.

17

2 WORKING OUT WORD MEANINGS

WORDS

GETTING THE IDEA

A test often asks you to figure out the meaning of a word given in a passage.

> Everything went wrong for Joanie last week. First her dog got sick, then she lost her after-school job. Finally, she tripped and broke her ankle. Despite everything, Joanie didn't complain. She stayed cheerful.
>
> Her friend Beth was impressed. "I don't think I could cope with all these problems the way you do," she said.

What does *cope* mean?

A   fall apart

B   deal with

C   forget

D   enjoy

How can you figure out the meaning of the word named in the question? You can use **context clues**.

Context clues are words in the same sentence as the word in question. They may also be found in other sentences before and after that word. All of these clues will help you understand how the chosen word is used in the passage.

Here is how you can use context clues to figure out the meaning of *cope* in the passage above:

1. **Read the sentence that contains the new word.** The way that *cope* is used in the last sentence indicates that it has to do with an action related to dealing with a problem.

2. **Read the sentences that surround the sentence with the new word.** They identify the kinds of problems Joanie had to deal with. These are important clues.

    NOTICE: Photocopying any part of this book is forbidden by law.

3. **Take a guess at what the new word means**. Try to think of a synonym for *cope*. From the context clues, you might guess that *cope* means "handle."

4. **Read all the answer choices. Cross out the ones you know or believe are wrong. Mark the choice closest to your guess**. Choices A, C, and D are not close in meaning to your guess, but answer Choice **B** is.

5. **Check back in the passage to be sure your choice makes sense**. The words *deal with* make sense in place of the word *cope*.

Now use context clues to answer the question in the next example.

Example 1

Jon hung up the phone and turned excitedly to speak to his friend.

"This is terrific!" shouted Jon. "Wait 'til you hear the news!"

"I've never seen you so elated," said Carlos. " Tell me what the wonderful news is that made you so happy."

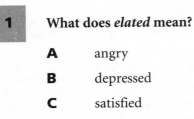 **1** **What does *elated* mean?**

    A   angry

    B   depressed

    C   satisfied

    D   thrilled

The selection tells you that Jon was happy and had wonderful news. Therefore, you can eliminate answer Choices A and B. Jon's words indicate that he is more than just satisfied, so Choice C is not the correct answer. The correct answer is Choice **D**.

NOTICE: Photocopying any part of this book is forbidden by law.

Some context clues are examples that help you understand a word's meaning. In the next example, you will read about someone being *cordial*. You are not asked what *cordial* means. Instead, you are asked to choose yet another example of cordial behavior.

Example 2

The salesperson smiled warmly at me as I explained I was looking for a gift for my sister. She listened as I explained what my sister liked. She showed me several things, then told me to take my time deciding. When I finally chose something, she chatted pleasantly as she wrapped the gift. I was pleased the store had such a cordial salesperson.

2   **Who else would be *cordial*?**

A   someone who pushes ahead of you on line

B   someone who enjoys shopping

C   someone who always says "Good Morning" and asks how you are doing

D   someone who ignores you when you say hello

From the context, you can tell that *cordial* means "friendly and warm." You can eliminate Choices A and D because these are rude behaviors and the salesperson was not rude. Choice B doesn't make sense because the salesperson was not shopping. The correct answer is Choice **C**. This is another example of cordial behavior.

 NOTICE: Photocopying any part of this book is forbidden by law.

PHRASES AND EXPRESSIONS

Sometimes the test asks you to figure out the meaning of a **phrase** or an **expression**. Both are groups of words that together mean something different from each individual word in the phrase or expression.

Use context clues to answer the questions in the next two examples.

Example 3

Jim shouldn't have climbed that shaky ladder to the roof. It was far too risky. He really took his life in his hands when he climbed up there. I was very relieved when he came down.

3   **What does *took his life in his hands* mean?**

- **A**   used his hands to do something
- **B**   hurt himself badly
- **C**   did something very dangerous
- **D**   shook hands with someone

The passage doesn't say Jim was hurt, or that he shook hands with someone, so you can eliminate answer Choices B and D right away. Using the context clues *shaky ladder to the roof* and *risky* should help you recognize that Jim did a dangerous thing. *Dangerous* is a synonym for *risky*, so the correct answer is Choice **C**.

Example 4

Mia always found something interesting in her grandparents' basement. Last week she found some pretty pearl buttons in a tin box. When she showed them to her grandfather, he said, "Oh, those are collar buttons. They were a dime a dozen when I was young. Everyone sold them and everyone used them. But no one has any use for them now." Mia didn't care if they were worthless now. She thought they were pretty, so she kept them.

NOTICE: Photocopying any part of this book is forbidden by law.

4 What does *a dime a dozen* mean?

   A something that is rare

   B something that is very expensive

   C something that is very common

   D something that is colorful

The context clues *Everyone sold them and everyone used them* should help you figure out that Choice **C** is the correct answer. The collar buttons were once very common. The other answer choices do not fit the meaning of the passage.

TIPS AND STRATEGIES
FOR WORKING OUT WORD MEANINGS

☛ You can use **context clues** to help you figure out what a word or phrase means. Context clues are:

  • other words in the *same* sentence as the chosen word, phrase or expression

  • other sentences surrounding the chosen word, phrase or expression

☛ To use context clues:

  • Read the sentence that contains the new word or phrase.

  • Read the sentences before and after this sentence.

  • Take a guess at what the new word or phrase probably means.

  • Read the answer choices. Cross out the ones you know or believe are wrong. Mark the choice closest to your guess.

  • Check back in the passage to make sure your choice makes sense.

   NOTICE: Photocopying any part of this book is forbidden by law.

SELECTIONS FOR PRACTICE

Selection 1

Poor Allen! This week he had one mishap after another. First, he tripped on his shoelace and fell down four steps. He banged his knee badly. Then, he hit his head on a low pipe in our basement. To top it off, he tripped up the steps when he was carrying the groceries into the house and broke half a dozen eggs. He got egg on his new shirt when he was cleaning up, too.

1   **What does *mishap* mean?**

    A   good fortune

    B   lucky event

    C   accident

    D   fall

Selection 2

There is a factory in our town that has been dumping waste products into a nearby stream for years. A citizen's group became alarmed when some wells downstream were found to contain one of the chemicals the factory uses. The group took the factory to court to stop the pollution, and won. The judge agreed that it was important to protect the purity of our drinking water.

2   **Which person is the most likely to be concerned with the *purity* of something?**

    A   someone collecting trash

    B   someone bandaging a cut

    C   someone riding a bicycle

    D   someone operating a machine

NOTICE: Photocopying any part of this book is forbidden by law.

Selection 3

At one time the Bronsons were quite wealthy. They were famous for their wonderful parties. They drove expensive cars. Then, about two years ago, Mr. Bronson lost a lot of money in the stock market. Next, he was laid off from his job and was out of work for six months. The Bronsons never told anyone. Although they couldn't afford it, they continued to give parties and to keep their expensive cars. Both thought it was important to keep up appearances.

3 **What does it mean to *keep up appearances*?**

A   make things look as if nothing has changed

B   have wonderful parties

C   drive expensive cars

D   admit they couldn't afford things

Selection 4

Brenda loves to grow things. She has a vegetable garden behind her house where she grows delicious tomatoes and beans. She has geraniums in a flower box on the front steps and beautiful house plants inside. She seems able to get plants to grow when no one else can. Everyone says she has a green thumb.

4 **What does it mean to have *a green thumb*?**

A   to paint one's thumb green

B   to like vegetables

C   to be good at growing things

D   to wear green nail polish`

NOTICE: Photocopying any part of this book is forbidden by law.

3 IDENTIFYING STATED INFORMATION

GETTING THE IDEA

Several questions on the test will ask you to identify a piece of information stated in a selection you read. A small piece of information about a topic or story is called a **detail**. A detail answers a *who*, *what*, *when*, *where*, *why*, or *how* question.

A detail question might look like the following:

> In the mid 1800s, most Irish peasants depended totally on the potato to feed their families. Then, in 1845, disaster struck when a blight, or disease, infected the potatoes. The potato crop failed several years in a row. Between 1845 and 1847, more than a million people died from starvation or disease. Many more left Ireland.

> **In what year did the blight hit the potato crop in Ireland?**
>
> **A**   1800
>
> **B**   1845
>
> **C**   1847
>
> **D**   1947

You don't have to guess the answer to a detail question. You can find the answer stated in the selection.

Here are some things you can do to help you find the correct piece of information:

1. **Read the question first and underline the key words**. The key words in the question above are *what year* and *blight*.

2. **Read the answer choices**. They name different years.

3. **Read the selection**. Look for the details that mention years.

NOTICE: Photocopying any part of this book is forbidden by law.

4. **Reread the question. Then find the part of the selection that has the information you are looking for**. The information you are looking for is in the second sentence of the passage.

5. **Find the answer choice that is most like the detail in the selection**. The correct answer is Choice **B**.

Use the steps you have learned to answer the following questions.

Example 1

In 1607, three small ships of the Virginia Company entered Chesapeake Bay. The English settlers on board were impressed with the land they saw. The newcomers chose a place near a large river. They called the river the James River, after England's King James I. In the next few weeks they built houses, a church, and a fort. These newcomers called their settlement Jamestown.

1   **The newcomers named the river after**

  A   the Virginia Company

  B   Jamestown

  C   King James I

  D   Chesapeake Bay

Did you underline the key words *newcomers*, *named*, and *river*? Next, you should have looked back to the passage for what the settlers named the river. The correct answer is Choice **C**.

NOTICE: Photocopying any part of this book is forbidden by law.

Example 2

Since the turn of the century, people have been fascinated with the idea of life on Mars. Fuzzy pictures through a telescope led some to believe they saw canals—inland waterways—on Mars. It also seemed as if Mars changed color from summer to winter.

In July 1965, *Mariner 4* transmitted 22 close-up photos of Mars. All that they showed was a surface pitted with craters and naturally occurring deeply grooved pathways. There was no evidence of artificial canals or flowing water.

2 **The *Mariner 4* photos showed**

    A   evidence of life in the soil of Mars

    B   fuzzy pictures of canals

    C   lots of plant growth

    D   a surface pitted with craters

The key words in the question are *Mariner 4* and *photos*. When you skim for these key words in the passage, you find the information in the second sentence of the second paragraph. Answer Choice **D** is correct.

Example 3

Martha checked her meager supply of food. She still had some cornmeal and a pumpkin, but the dried berries and salted fish were gone. She had finished the last of the rabbit stew a week ago. Now hunger was gnawing at her stomach. And although Martha was a good hunter herself, she did not like hunting by herself.

Martha finally admitted her worry to herself. It had been three weeks since her father had left on a hunting trip. He had never stayed away more than two weeks before. Had something happened to him?

NOTICE: Photocopying any part of this book is forbidden by law.

3   **Why was Martha worried?**

    A   Her father had finished the rabbit stew.

    B   She was a good hunter.

    C   She only had some cornmeal and a pumpkin left.

    D   Her father had been gone for three weeks.

Did you underline the key words *why*, *Martha*, and *worried*? You can find the word *worry* in the second paragraph. The next two sentences give you the information. Choice **D** is the correct answer.

TIPS AND STRATEGIES
FOR IDENTIFYING STATED INFORMATION

☛ Remember that a **detail** is a small piece of information stated in a selection. It may be a fact about a topic. It may be a detail about a character, place, or event in a story.

☛ You don't have to guess the answer to a detail question. You can look back in the selection to find the correct piece of information.

☛ To answer a detail question:

- Read the question first and underline the key words. This helps you to know what kind of fact or story detail you need to look for. Read the answer choices. Then read the selection.

- Reread the question. Then find the part of the selection that has the information you are looking for. Reread this part of the selection.

- Reread each answer choice to find the one that is most like the fact or story detail stated in the selection.

 NOTICE: Photocopying any part of this book is forbidden by law.

SELECTIONS FOR PRACTICE

Selection 1

The power of volcanoes has always fascinated and terrified people. Volcanoes are openings in the Earth's surface from which lava, hot gases, and bits of rock erupt with great force. However, volcanoes begin deep within the Earth. The heat is so great at certain depths that rock melts. This melted rock is called magma. As the rock melts, a gas also forms, and this gas-filled magma rises slowly upward. Eventually the magma and gas find a passageway to the surface.

Sometimes the magma finds an opening and simply seeps from the ground. Often, however, by the time the magma and gas find their way to the surface, a great deal of pressure has built up. The gas and magma blast out and a volcanic eruption occurs.

Once the magma has reached the surface, it is called lava. The lava is red-hot when it erupts from the opening, but it cools and hardens as it flows and finally turns into rock. The volcano grows larger as more volcanic rock accumulates.

1A **What is the magma called when it reaches the surface?**

    A   melted rock

    B   lava

    C   a volcanic eruption

    D   gaseous magma

1B **What state is volcanic rock in when it settles?**

    A   hot, gaseous magma

    B   red-hot lava

    C   watery magma

    D   cool, hardened lava

NOTICE: Photocopying any part of this book is forbidden by law.

29

Selection 2

Carol and Miko had been friends since they were in elementary school. They both loved to ice skate, and they usually went to the gym together. Sometimes they ran in the morning before school, too. But for the past week, every time Carol came by her house, Miko said she didn't feel like going to the gym. She told Carol she just didn't have time for ice skating. Carol wouldn't think of asking Miko to play a board game. She knew Miko didn't enjoy them.

Carol wondered what was wrong. On Saturday she went for a run alone. It was her birthday, and she was hurt that Miko hadn't called her like she had always done in the past. Somehow the presents from her family weren't enough.

That evening her mother asked her to go with her to pick up some food at a restaurant. When they got to the restaurant, Carol opened the door and went in. "Surprise!" yelled Miko and about five of Carol's friends.

"I knew I wouldn't be able to keep the surprise a secret if I saw you this week," Miko explained. Both girls had a good laugh.

2A **What did Carol and Miko NOT do together?**

A   run

B   go to the gym

C   ice skate

D   play board games

2B **Why was Carol feeling hurt?**

A   Miko hadn't called on Carol's birthday.

B   Miko liked to go to the gym.

C   Miko went for a run alone.

D   Miko didn't want to go to the restaurant.

 NOTICE: Photocopying any part of this book is forbidden by law.

4 IDENTIFYING SEQUENCE OF EVENTS

GETTING THE IDEA

A **sequence of events** is the **order** in which things happen. This order is time order—what happens *first*, *next*, *then*, and *last*. Events are usually told or written in time order so that we can easily follow them.

A question on the test about sequence might look like the one below.

> Jane woke up early and jumped out of bed. First, she brushed her teeth and showered. Then she got dressed in her favorite shorts and T-shirt. Next, she went to the kitchen and ate a big bowl of cereal and milk. She grabbed her beach bag and finally dashed out the door.

What happened last?

A   Jane dashed out the door.

B   Jane got dressed.

C   Jane brushed her teeth and showered.

D   Jane ate breakfast.

Here is what you can you do to answer a sequence question.

1. **Read the question. Underline key words such as *first*, *after*, and *last*.** The key word in the question in the box above is *last*.

2. **Read the answer choices. Then read the selection.** In the passage above, you will find the key words *first*, *then*, *next*, and *finally*. They are clues to the time order of the events.

3. **Go back to the selection to find the correct event.** When you use the time clues in the selection to follow the order of events, you discover that the last event is that Jane dashed out the door. The correct answer is Choice **A**. The other events happened before Jane left her house.

Use the steps you learned to answer the sequence question below.

Example 1

At first, Eduardo was nervous about the job interview. He was worried about what he would say. Then, when he arrived at the office and met the interviewer, he began to relax. He answered the questions with ease. Finally, after it was over, Eduardo was exhilarated. He felt sure he'd get the job.

1 **What happened last?**

A Eduardo was nervous.

B Eduardo was sure he'd get the job.

C Eduardo worried about what to say.

D Eduardo arrived at the office.

Did you underline the word *last* in the question? The word *finally* is a synonym for *last*. So the correct answer is Choice **B**.

Sometimes a selection has few or no sequence clue words. Then you need to find the events in the selection that happened before and after the event asked for in the question. Decide which event answers the question.

Example 2

Tania was only up for a few minutes when she knew something was wrong. Her head ached and she felt weak. She thought she might feel better if she ate something, so she walked down the street to the coffee shop. But as soon as she smelled the food, she knew she wasn't hungry.

2 **Which event happened after Tania felt weak?**

A Tania couldn't say a word.

B Tania walked to the coffee shop.

C Tania woke up.

D Tania realized she wasn't hungry.

After you find the sentence that says Tania felt weak, you find that the next event is that she walked down the street to the coffee shop. So the correct answer is Choice **B**.

 NOTICE: Photocopying any part of this book is forbidden by law.

USING A CHART TO UNDERSTAND SEQUENCE

Sometimes a test may ask you to complete a sequence chart based on a selection. One kind of sequence chart has boxes with arrows. Events are placed in each box, from left to right to show the order of events.

Example 3

Sometimes a plant outgrows its pot. To repot a plant, first, choose a new pot, one or two inches larger than the pot the plant is in now. Put a stone or a piece of broken pottery over the hole in the bottom and add a little potting soil.

Next, water the plant well. Turn the pot over and tap it sharply. Slip the plant, root ball and all, out of the old pot. Put the plant into the new pot and fill in the space with fresh potting soil. Finally water the plant again to settle the soil.

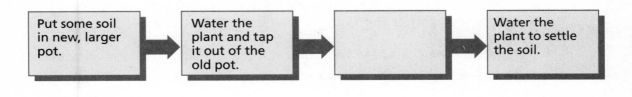

| Put some soil in new, larger pot. | → | Water the plant and tap it out of the old pot. | → | | → | Water the plant to settle the soil. |

3 **What belongs in the empty box?**

A Don't water the plant until it's in the new pot.

B Turn the pot over and tap it sharply.

C Get a new, larger pot.

D Put the plant into the new pot and add fresh soil.

The correct answer is Choice **D**. Answer Choice A has the wrong information. The events listed for Choices B and C happen before you put the plant into the new pot and add soil.

NOTICE: Photocopying any part of this book is forbidden by law.

TIPS AND STRATEGIES
FOR IDENTIFYING SEQUENCE OF EVENTS

☛ Remember that the **sequence of events** is the **order** in which things happen. When you understand the order of events, you know what happened *first*, what happened *next*, what happened *then*, and so on.

☛ To identify the correct event for a sequence question:

- Read the question first and underline key words such as *first*, *last*, *before*, and *after*. Read the answer choices.

- Read the selection. If key words such as *first*, *next*, *then*, *before*, and *after* appear in the selection, use them to help you follow the order of events. If these word clues do not appear, follow the sequence as best you can.

- Reread the question and answer choices.

- Go back to the selection and find the event asked for or described in the question. Use the key words to find the correct event. If there are few or no key words in the selection, reread the sentences before and after the event named in the question.

☛ Sequence charts can help you understand a sequence. Read a sequence chart from left to right.

NOTICE: Photocopying any part of this book is forbidden by law.

SELECTIONS FOR PRACTICE

Selection 1

The hurricane had occurred in September, but it was already November and Francesca hadn't received the insurance money yet.

She didn't understand what the problem was. Francesca had called the insurance company, obtained the forms, filled them out, and sent in all the paperwork. Then she had called a contractor, who had started repairing her roof.

If she didn't get the money soon, she wouldn't be able to pay the contractor. She decided to call the insurance company again and speak to her insurance agent.

1A   **What did Francesca do first after the hurricane had hit?**

    A   She started repairing her roof.

    B   She called the contractor.

    C   She called the insurance company.

    D   She filled out the insurance forms.

1B   **What happened before Francesca hired a contractor?**

    A   She called the insurance company again.

    B   She filled out the forms and sent in the paperwork.

    C   She received a check from the insurance company.

    D   She fixed the roof herself.

NOTICE: Photocopying any part of this book is forbidden by law.

Selection 2

You can make a simple book to use as a sketch book or notebook. First, take four to six sheets of good quality, unlined paper and stack them together. Fold the sheets in half and crease the folds sharply. Next, thread a sharp needle with strong, white thread. Sew down the center of the folded pages through all the sheets, using stitches about a half-inch long. Tie off the thread.

Now open up your book. If you like, you can make a cover. Then enjoy using your very own book!

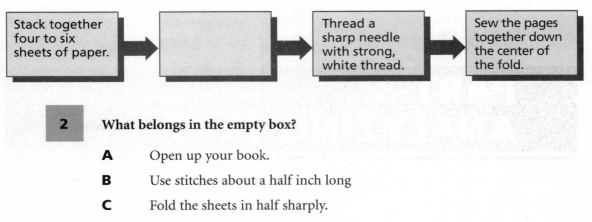

Stack together four to six sheets of paper. → ☐ → Thread a sharp needle with strong, white thread. → Sew the pages together down the center of the fold.

2 **What belongs in the empty box?**

A Open up your book.

B Use stitches about a half inch long

C Fold the sheets in half sharply.

D Tie off the thread.

NOTICE: Photocopying any part of this book is forbidden by law.

PART 3:
ANALYZING TEXT

NOTICE: Photocopying any part of this book is forbidden by law.

5 IDENTIFYING CAUSE AND EFFECT

GETTING THE IDEA

When you read, it is important to understand connections between people, ideas, and events so you can make sense of them. One important kind of connection to look for is **cause and effect**. The **cause** happens first. It is the reason why something else happens. What happens as a result is the **effect**.

The test asks several questions about causes. A passage may have the word *because* in it to let you know that the reason is directly stated.

In 1632, George Calvert, later called Lord Baltimore, was given land by King Charles I of England. Calvert planned to start a colony in the New World north of Chesapeake Bay. The first colonists arrived in 1634. Many of the colonists were Catholics, as was Calvert. They wanted to leave England because Protestants there often treated Catholics unfairly.

1 **Why did Calvert and other Catholics leave England?**

  A   They didn't like King Charles I.

  B   They wanted to be Protestants.

  C   They arrived in 1634.

  D   Protestants there often treated Catholics unfairly.

Often a passage on a test does not have the clue word *because*. The question, however, will contain the word *because*.

Marilla and Janie went to the movies on Thursday. Janie laughed at the silly jokes and tapped her feet to the music. Marilla laughed a few times, but she soon began to squirm in her seat. To her, the movie seemed endless. Finally it was over and time to leave. "Didn't you like the movie?" asked Janie. "I guess I just don't like musicals," Marilla answered.

2 **Marilla didn't enjoy the movie because**

  A   she didn't like the seats

  B   she didn't like musicals

  C   she didn't understand the plot

  D   she didn't like the jokes

    NOTICE: Photocopying any part of this book is forbidden by law.

Here is what you can you do to find a cause-and-effect connection:

1. **Read the question. Underline key words such as *why* and *because*. These words are clues that you need to look in the passage for a cause. Each of these words are in the questions on page 38.**

2. **Read the passage. See if it has the key word *because*. If it does, the words after the key word will explain why something happened.** In the last sentence of the first passage, the words that follow *because* explain why Calvert and other Catholics left England in 1634.

3. **If the passage does not have the word *because*, ask yourself, "What happened?" Then ask, "Why did it happen?"** The second passage does not have the word *because*. You learn that Marilla squirmed in her seat as she watched the movie musical. Ask yourself, "Why did this happen?"

4. **Read over the question and the answer choices. Decide on an answer. Check it in the passage.** The correct answer to question 1 is answer Choice **D**. The information appears in the last sentence of the passage. The answer to question 2 is in the last sentence of the passage. The correct answer is Choice **B**.

Use the steps you learned to find the cause and effect connections in Examples 1–3.

Example 1

Petroleum has been used for thousands of years. Because oil keeps out air and moisture, the Egyptians used it to coat mummies and thus preserve the bodies. Petroleum was also used as a waterproof coating on early roads. In the early 1800s, petroleum was used in medicines. By the late 1840s, people learned something new about oil. It could be used to make the fuel kerosene.

1 **Why did the Egyptians use oil to coat their mummies?**

   A   No other product was available.

   B   It was useful for making the fuel kerosene.

   C   The oil kept air and moisture away from the bodies.

   D   The oil made early roads waterproof.

The information is directly stated in the second sentence of the passage, after the word *because*: The correct answer is Choice **C**.

- -
NOTICE: Photocopying any part of this book is forbidden by law.   **39**

Example 2

Jason sighed and wiped his forehead. He took a drink of water from his water bottle. Mowing the lawn was hard work on a hot day like this. But he kept going when he thought of the money he was earning.

"This is the third lawn this week," he thought. "Three times twenty is sixty dollars. By the end of the summer I'll have earned enough to buy the new speakers for my guitar."

Jason restarted the lawn mower to finish the last section of grass.

2 **Why was Jason mowing the lawn?**

A   His father asked him to do it.

B   He enjoyed doing it.

C   He was earning money to buy new speakers.

D   He liked being outdoors.

The word *because* is not in the passage; but Jason's thoughts in the second paragraph explains what he wants to do with the money he is earning—to buy new speakers for his guitar. Choice **C** is the correct answer.

Example 3

In 1962, a woman named Rachel Carson published an important book called *Silent Spring*. In her book, Carson rang an alarm bell. There were fewer and fewer songbirds to welcome in the spring each year, she said in her book. The reason, Carson explained, was the use of the pesticide DDT. Carson's book stirred people's concern about the environment.

3 **According to Carson, there were fewer and fewer songbirds because**

A   a book called *Silent Spring* was published

B   a pesticide called DDT was being sprayed

C   there were too many other kinds of birds

D   an alarm bell sounded loudly all the time

Clues to the correct answer are in the fourth sentence of the selection. Choice **B** is the correct answer.

     NOTICE: Photocopying any part of this book is forbidden by law.

USING A CHART TO UNDERSTAND CAUSE AND EFFECT

Sometimes a test asks you to complete a cause-and-effect chart based on a selection. A cause-and-effect chart shows the cause (reason) in one column of the chart and the effect (result) in another column. You read the chart from left to right.

Example 4

Alison taught elementary school. She was also a painter. Ever since she'd studied French in high school she had wanted to visit France. She'd read about the wonderful art museums there. She longed to see them for herself and to spend time painting the French countryside, too.

Alison began to plan a trip to France for her next summer vacation. She knew she would need to speak French on her trip. Because she didn't remember much of the language from her high school classes, she decided to take a night school class in French. So she signed up for a French class at the local college.

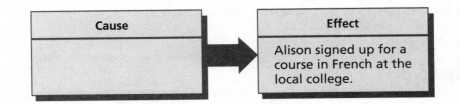

Cause	Effect
	Alison signed up for a course in French at the local college.

4 **What belongs in the empty box?**

A   Alison wanted to teach elementary school.

B   Alison didn't remember much French from high school.

C   Alison wanted to teach French next year.

D   Alison had a friend who went to the college.

The chart shows the effect, or what happened. The cause, or reason, follows the word *because* in the third sentence of the second paragraph: *she didn't remember much of the language from her high school classes*. The correct answer is Choice **B**.

- -

NOTICE: Photocopying any part of this book is forbidden by law.

Here is another example with a chart. However, this passage and chart show more than one effect for a cause.

Example 5

For thousands of years, the Lakota and other people of the Great Plains lived in villages along rivers. The people lived in lodges made of logs covered with grass and soil. They were farmers. In the summer, the men left the village to hunt buffalo. They returned in the fall to harvest their crops.

In the 1500s, the Spanish came to North America, bringing horses with them. In time, some of these horses ran away and formed wild herds on the Plains. By the 1700s the Lakota were taming these horses.

Having horses brought great changes to the Lakota's way of life. They used them to hunt buffalo. Buffalo meat replaced farming as the Lakota' s main source of food. In addition, many Lakota stopped living in permanent villages. Instead they moved from one campsite to another, following the buffalo herds.

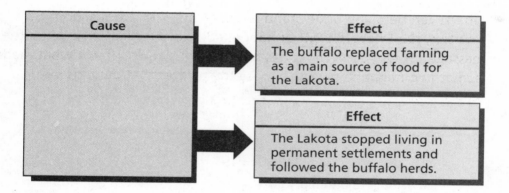

Cause		Effect
	→	The buffalo replaced farming as a main source of food for the Lakota.
	→	**Effect** The Lakota stopped living in permanent settlements and followed the buffalo herds.

5 **What belongs in the empty box?**

    A   The Lakota lived in villages along streams.

    B   The Lakota lived by farming and hunting.

    C   The Lakota tamed wild horses.

    D   The Lakota got tired of living in lodges.

Your teacher will discuss your answer.

NOTICE: Photocopying any part of this book is forbidden by law.

TIPS AND STRATEGIES
FOR IDENTIFYING CAUSE AND EFFECT

☛ Remember that a **cause** is the reason why something happens. An **effect** is what happens.

☛ **To find a cause-and-effect connection:**

- Read the question first. Look for and **underline key words** such as *why* and *because*. They signal that you need to look in the passage for a reason that something happened.

- Read the selection. Look for the key word *because*. The words that follow it will give the reason why something happened.

- If there are no key words, ask yourself **"What happened?"** Then ask **"Why did it happen?"** Find the answers in the passage.

- Reread the question and answer choices.

- Reread the selection and find the event asked for or described in the question.

☛ Charts can help you understand a cause-and-effect connection. On the test, the **Effect** box (what happened) is often filled in. Look in the passage for why something has happened. Once you know what made something happen, you can choose the answer that belongs in the **Cause** box.

NOTICE: Photocopying any part of this book is forbidden by law.

SELECTIONS FOR PRACTICE

Selection 1

Sometimes after a big storm, beaches are covered with dead fish, seaweed, broken shells, and pieces of wood. Most seaweed is brown or gold, but there are often pieces of white seaweed. If people visit the beaches, the white seaweed disappears very quickly. White seaweed makes a delicious pudding.

1 **White seaweed probably disappears quickly because**

    A   it is picked up by people and cooked

    B   it floats out to sea

    C   it gets tangled up in the broken shells

    D   it gets blown away by the storm

Selection 2

Elena loved to skate and she was very good at it. She practiced long hours before and after school every day. In fact, she usually woke at 4 AM. After a quick breakfast, one of her parents would drive her to the ice rink near her home, and she would practice for two hours. Then, she would leave for school. After school, Elena would skate for another two hours before doing her homework.

Elena sometimes got tired of her demanding schedule, but to her it was worth it. Her goal was to win an Olympic medal someday; and she knew hard work was the only way to become a champion skater.

2 **Elena kept up her demanding schedule because**

    A   she liked to get up early

    B   she didn't want to do homework

    C   she liked having a schedule

    D   she wanted to become a champion skater

    NOTICE: Photocopying any part of this book is forbidden by law.

Selection 3

In 1862, Congress passed the Pacific Railroad Act. This act offered two companies government loans to build a railroad across the continent. Seven years later, the task was accomplished. It was now possible to travel from coast to coast by railroad. This transcontinental railroad made it possible for people and goods to travel from New York to San Francisco in a little over a week. More and more people began to move West, and even more railroads were built.

But the railroads came at a cost, too. The Native Americans of the Great Plains, who had built their lives around the buffalo herds, lost their way of life forever.

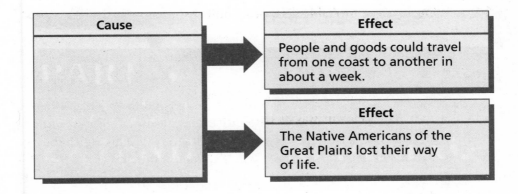

Cause	Effect
	People and goods could travel from one coast to another in about a week.
	Effect
	The Native Americans of the Great Plains lost their way of life.

3 **What belongs in the empty box?**

A Native Americans hunted the buffalo.

B More and more people moved West.

C Companies received government loans.

D A railroad was completed that stretched from coast to coast.

NOTICE: Photocopying any part of this book is forbidden by law.

6 COMPARING AND CONTRASTING

People often speak and write about how two or more things are alike or different. On the test you will find questions that ask you how two people, events, or even whole passages are alike or different. When you analyze how things are alike, you are **comparing** them. When you analyze how things are different, you are **contrasting** them.

This example asks you to **compare** two Native American nations. Look for ways they are the same.

> The Navajo live in the dry regions of the American Southwest. The Navajo raise sheep and grow crops of corn, beans, squash, and melons. They weave fine rugs from the wool of their sheep. Also important is silversmithing, which the Navajo learned from Mexican craftspeople in the nineteenth century.
>
> The Hopi live in the Southwest, too. Like the Navajo, they also raise sheep and grow corn. The Hopi are also silversmiths and are known for their beautiful jewelry.

1　**How are the Hopi and the Navajo alike?**

　　A　　Both nations live in the Souththeast.

　　B　　Both nations are known for the beautiful rugs they weave.

　　C　　Both nations are fine silversmiths.

　　D　　Both nations raise beans, squash, and melons.

This example asks you to **contrast** two people.

> Marissa and Juliet are sisters. Marissa is very friendly and outgoing, and people can get to know her easily. Her sister Juliet, however, is more reserved. She is harder to know. People sometimes think Juliet is unfriendly, but she is really very shy.

2　**What is one way Marissa and Juliet differ?**

　　A　　Marissa is reserved.

　　B　　Juliet is outgoing.

　　C　　The girls are sisters.

　　D　　Juliet is harder to know than Marissa.

 NOTICE: Photocopying any part of this book is forbidden by law.

You can take the following steps to answer a compare or contrast question:

1. **Underline key words in the question**. A key word such as *alike* or *different* tells you whether to compare or contrast. Question 1 on page 46 has the key word *alike*, which tells you to compare. Question 2 has the key word *differ*, which tells you to contrast.

2. **Read the selection. Look for the same kind of key words found in the question. Key words such as *same*, *alike*, *also*, and *both* are used to compare**. Key words such as *different*, *unlike*, *but*, and *however* are used to contrast. The compare key word in the first passage is *also*. The contrast key word in the second passage is *however*.

3. **Remember that some sentences may not have a key word like the ones listed above**. You may find other kinds of words in passages that contrast, such as *larger*, *smaller*, *higher*, and *lower*.

4. **Reread the question and the answer choices. Go back to the passage and find the information you need**. Choice **C** is the answer to question 1. Choice **D** is the answer to question 2.

Now read and answer the following examples.

Example 1

Both foxes and wolves are members of the dog family. Foxes usually live and hunt alone; however, wolves live and hunt in packs. The pack is led by the strongest male and female. The entire pack helps raise the pups. Young wolves may stay with the pack for several years. Foxes only come together as a pair to raise pups. But when young foxes are able to hunt on their own, the family group breaks up and the young foxes leave the territory.

1 **One way foxes and wolves differ is**

    A   the wolf is a member of the dog family and hunts alone

    B   the fox is a good hunter and stays with the pack

    C   wolves live and hunt in packs, and foxes do not

    D   wolves do not raise pups

The correct answer is Choice **C**. The key word *however* in the second sentence of the passage helps you find the information about the different way that foxes and wolves live and hunt.

NOTICE: Photocopying any part of this book is forbidden by law.

Example 2

Well-known author Jean Craighead George wrote both *Julie of the Wolves* and *My Side of the Mountain*. The two books are wilderness survival stories with teenage heroes. Each main character displays a deep respect for animals and the environment.

In each story, the hero lives off the land. The land in *Julie of the Wolves* is the Arctic tundra. In *My Side of the Mountain*, the land is the Catskill Mountains of New York state.

2 **What is one way in which *Julie of the Wolves* and *My Side of the Mountain* are similar?**

   A   They are both wilderness survival stories.

   B   They both take place in the Arctic tundra.

   C   They both take place in New York State.

   D   They both have female main characters.

The information you need to answer the question is in the first paragraph of the passage. The correct answer is Choice **A**.

Example 3

At first glance, Marla and Jessie did not seem alike at all. Marla was tall and slim, while Jessie was shorter and a little plump. Jessie was talkative, and Marla was quieter. Both girls enjoyed reading and discussing mystery novels, and they loved the outdoors. They often went on rafting trips or hikes together.

3 **How were Marla and Jessie alike?**

   A   Both girls were talkative.

   B   Both girls loved the outdoors.

   C   Neither girl liked rafting.

   D   The girls looked alike.

The fourth sentence begins with the key word *both*. This should alert you to expect to read ways in which the girls *are alike*. Choice **B** is the correct answer.

   NOTICE: Photocopying any part of this book is forbidden by law.

USING A CHART TO COMPARE AND CONTRAST

Sometimes a test question will ask you to complete a chart that compares and contrasts two people or things. You read a passage first, and then use the information to complete the chart. You read the chart from left to right.

Example 4

Ted's mother had decided to buy another car, but she was having a hard time making up her mind between two cars she had seen. One car was a small red station wagon with 4-wheel drive. It got great gas mileage, but it was three years old and had a lot of miles on it. The second car was a sporty blue sedan. It had front-wheel drive and was only a year old. However, it did not get very many miles for each gallon of gas. Both were about the same price—$6,000.

Ted's mother decided to make a chart to organize the information about the two cars.

Red Station Wagon	Blue Sedan
4-wheel drive	front-wheel drive
3 years old	1 year old
good gas mileage	
selling for $6,000	selling for $6,000

4 **What belongs in the empty box?**

  A   same price

  B   sporty

  C   gas mileage not good

  D   had a lot of miles on it

If you read across each row of the chart, you can see the ways in which the cars are different and the one way in which the cars are alike. Since the empty box is across from the words *good gas mileage* under the Red Station Wagon heading, you need to check in the passage to find the information about what kind of mileage the blue sedan gets. This information is found towards the end of the first paragraph. The correct answer is Choice **C**.

- - - - - - - - - - - - - - - - - - -

NOTICE: Photocopying any part of this book is forbidden by law.

Sometimes the test may ask you to complete another kind of chart called a **Venn diagram**. The outer circles show differences between two things. The middle circle shows similarities.

Example 5

There are many kinds of bagpipes, but the two best-known are the Scottish, or Highland, bagpipe and the Irish bagpipe. Both bagpipes consist of a bag with several pipes that contain reeds. For the Highland bagpipe, the player blows air through the blowpipe to inflate the bag. Then the player squeezes the bag to force air out through the other pipes. This kind of bagpipe has four reeds that vibrate to create the sound. The Highland pipes are played standing and are best played outdoors.

The Irish pipes are not blown by mouth. Instead, the player uses an elbow to work a bellows tied to the waist. The bellows pumps air into the bag. The player then squeezes the bag with the other arm to force air through the pipes. The Irish pipes contain eight reeds. Unlike the Highland pipes, the Irish pipes are played sitting down and are meant for indoor use.

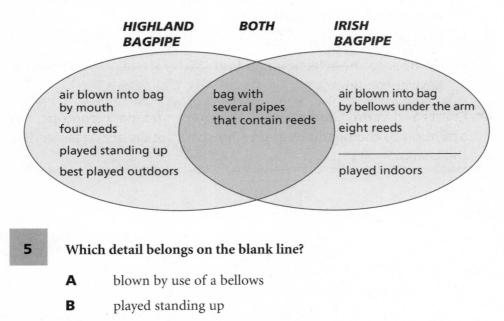

5   **Which detail belongs on the blank line?**

    A   blown by use of a bellows

    B   played standing up

    C   also called Scottish bagpipe

    D   played sitting down

The blank line is under **Irish bagpipe**. So look for a detail that points out a difference between the **Highland bagpipe** and the **Irish bagpipe**. The **Highland bagpipe** section of the diagram lists *played standing up*. So the correct answer under **Irish bagpipe** is Choice **D**, *played sitting down*. You can find this information in the last sentence of the passage.

NOTICE: Photocopying any part of this book is forbidden by law.

TIPS AND STRATEGIES
FOR COMPARING AND CONTRASTING

☞ Remember that when you tell how two or more things are alike, you are **comparing**. When you tell how two or more things are different, you are **contrasting**.

☞ To compare or contrast:

- Read the question first. To know if you are to compare or contrast, **underline key words** in the question. Key words such as *same*, *alike*, *also*, and *too* are words that signal comparison. Key words such as *different*, *unlike*, *but*, and *however* are words that signal contrast.

- Read the selection. Look for the same kinds of key words in the selection that you saw in the question.

- Remember that not every sentence will have a key word like the ones listed above. You may see other kinds of words that signal compare or contrast, such as *longer*, *shorter*, *more*, and *less*. Pay attention to these words as well.

- Reread the question and answer choices.

- Go back to the selection and find the information you need to answer the question.

☞ Charts and Venn diagrams can help you compare and contrast. Pay attention to the headings and to how the details are organized in the charts.

NOTICE: Photocopying any part of this book is forbidden by law.

SELECTIONS FOR PRACTICE

Selection 1

In the pre-Civil War South, a small number of white people owned large plantations. The profits from cotton made it possible for the owners to live lives of wealth and leisure. While slaves worked their land, the wealthy white landowners dressed in the latest fashion and gave big parties.

The majority of southern white people were poor. Most of them lived in log houses, often without glass windows. They had small farms on poorer land. Instead of cotton, they grew corn and vegetables. They might have a cow or two. The poor southern white people worked the land themselves. Despite this, they were in agreement with the wealthy plantation owners about the institution of slavery.

1 **How were the poor white southerners similar to the wealthy plantation owners?**

   A They dressed in the latest fashion.

   B They lived in mansions.

   C They could not afford slaves.

   D They supported the idea of slavery.

Selection 2

Bess enjoyed visiting her aunt in Ireland. Her aunt lived in the small village of Drumville, in a two-story house on the village's main street. In fact, the entire village had only a few streets. There were four or five village shops, including two grocery stores, a gas station, and a post office.

If anyone wanted to buy anything not sold in these shops, they had to go to Ennistown, about ten miles away. It had a larger main street with dozens of stores. Just on the outskirts of the town was a big shopping mall. There were restaurants and fast-food places, a bus station and a train station, too.

2 **How did Ennistown differ from Drumville?**

   A It was smaller.

   B It had more stores and a big shopping mall.

   C There was no train station.

   D There was no bus station.

 NOTICE: Photocopying any part of this book is forbidden by law.

Selection 3

The Suarez family disagreed on where to go on vacation. Mr. Suarez and Lisa wanted to go to the seashore at Cape Cod. They pointed out that there were beaches, and they could go sailing, too. There were places of historical interest to see and wonderful seafood restaurants.

But Yolanda and Mrs. Suarez preferred to visit the city of Boston. The hotel had a swimming pool, if anyone wanted to swim. There were many sites of historical interest and wonderful seafood as well.

The family compromised. They spent a few days in the city of Boston and then went to Cape Cod for a long weekend!

Cape Cod	Boston
beaches	hotel swimming pool
historical places of interest	historical places of interest
good seafood restaurants	

3 **What belongs in the empty box?**

A deep-sea fishing

B swimming

C shopping

D good seafood restaurants

NOTICE: Photocopying any part of this book is forbidden by law.

7 DRAWING CONCLUSIONS

GETTING THE IDEA

Some questions on the test ask you to find details directly stated in a selection. To answer other questions, you have to "read between the lines," because not all the information is stated directly. You have to combine your own knowledge and experience with information in the text to figure out what the author suggests. This is called **drawing a conclusion**.

To draw a conclusion about something in a nonfiction passage, combine the facts with your knowledge and experience.

To draw a conclusion about something in a fiction passage, combine details about characters, human behavior, and places with your knowledge and experience. Here is an example:

> Leslie smiled when she awoke on her day off and saw the clear sky. Quickly she dressed and ate. Then she grabbed her easel, her paints, and the lunch she had prepared the night before. Finally she had an entire day off to do nothing but paint! She could hardly wait to get to her favorite spot in the park.

How does Leslie probably feel about painting?

A   She'd rather do something else.

B   She only paints when she has to.

C   She loves to paint and looks forward to it.

D   She does not like to paint at all.

    NOTICE: Photocopying any part of this book is forbidden by law.

Use the following steps to answer questions that ask you to draw conclusions:

1. **Look for key words in the question to see what is being asked**. In the question on page 54, the word *probably* is the key word. It is a clue that you will have to figure out how Leslie feels about painting.

2. **Read the passage**. Look for information about what Leslie did on her day off.

3. **Reread the question and answer choices**. **Think about the details in the passage and what you already know from your own life**. The passage tells you that Leslie grabbed her easel, her paints, and the lunch she had prepared the night before. The passage also says that she could hardly wait to get to her favorite spot in the park. You know that these are all ways that people act when they enjoy an activity and look forward to doing it. So you can conclude that the best answer is Choice **C**.

Now try the next example.

Example 1

Marquette and Joliet were Frenchmen who lived in the late 1600s. They had heard of the great Mississippi River, which flowed west and then south from Lake Michigan. At this time, many explorers were looking for a "Northwest Passage," a waterway they hoped would lead west to the Pacific Ocean. Marquette and Joliet hoped the Mississippi would be it. They followed the Mississippi River until they came to the Arkansas River. There they saw that the Mississippi flowed south, not west. They decided to turn back to Lake Michigan.

3   **Marquette and Joliet probably thought that**

   A   the Mississippi was not the Northwest Passage

   B   Lake Michigan was the Northwest Passage

   C   the Arkansas River was the Northwest Passage

   D   the Mississippi was the Northwest Passage

The passage explains that Marquette and Joliet were looking for a waterway that flowed west. When they saw that the Mississippi flowed south, they realized that it was not the Northwest Passage. Answer Choice **A** is correct.

NOTICE: Photocopying any part of this book is forbidden by law.

After you draw a conclusion, another test question might ask you to choose a fact or story detail that supports that conclusion. Or you might be asked to identify which fact or story detail is *not* supporting evidence. You will need to go back to the selection to find the supporting evidence in order to determine the correct answer.

Example 2

The ancient kings of Egypt were powerful rulers. They built for themselves elaborate tombs that took many years to complete. After a pharaoh died, the body was carefully preserved and buried in a beautiful casket with many possessions. Bowls of food, amusements, clothing, chariots, even servants, were buried with the pharaoh. After the body was placed in the burial chamber, the entrance was carefully sealed.

2A **What might best explain why the ancient Egyptians buried so many things with their pharaoh?**

A The ancient Egyptians were rich.

B The ancient Egyptians believed in the afterlife.

C The ancient Egyptians all had many servants.

D The ancient Egyptians were afraid to die.

The question contains the key words *might best explain*. Information about what was buried with the pharaoh can help you figure out the best answer. The answer that makes the most sense is Choice **B**.

Now read this question about the same passage:

2B **Which detail from the passage does NOT support the answer for question 2A?**

A The pharaoh's body was preserved in a beautiful casket.

B Bowls of food and clothing were buried with the pharaoh.

C Servants were also buried with the pharaoh.

D The ancient Egyptians were powerful rulers.

The correct answer is Choice **D**. It is the only statement that does *not* support the conclusion for question 2.

NOTICE: Photocopying any part of this book is forbidden by law.

TIPS AND STRATEGIES
FOR DRAWING CONCLUSIONS

☛ Remember that you will not always find the answer to a test question stated directly in a selection. So you must **draw a conclusion** based on the information in the passage and on your own experience and knowledge.

☛ If the selection is nonfiction, the clues will be facts. If the selection is fiction, the clues will be story details.

☛ To draw a conclusion:

- Read the question first. Look for key words to see what is being asked. Key words like *probably*, *most likely*, and *not true* might be clues that you will have to draw a conclusion.

- Read the selection.

- Reread the question and answer choices.

- Use facts or story details and what you know to choose the answer that makes the most sense.

☛ After you draw a conclusion, another question may ask you to choose a fact or detail that supports your conclusion. In that case, reread the passage to find the correct fact or detail.

NOTICE: Photocopying any part of this book is forbidden by law.

SELECTIONS FOR PRACTICE

Selection 1

Justin had been playing chess since he was eight years old. He was in a chess club and he played against his friends whenever he could. He played a computer chess game, too. Once in a while Justin might play soccer or football with his brother Tad. Most of the time, however, Justin would meet a friend for a game of chess, or else he'd read a book about chess strategy.

1 **Which of the following is most likely true?**

 A   Tad was good at soccer.

 B   Justin didn't have any friends.

 C   Justin enjoyed chess more than playing sports.

 D   Tad didn't know how to play chess.

Selection 2

Early in the twentieth century, few scientists suspected that there was a world of living plants and animals on the bottom of the ocean. All known ocean life was dependent on the energy of the sun to live and grow. The sun was the greatest power source.

Beginning in 1977, scientists began to discover that volcanic springs on the bottom of the ocean were the source of energy for totally different forms of life. These volcanic sources produced a chemical called hydrogen sulfide, a substance that smells like rotten eggs and is poisonous to most life forms. But down on the ocean bottom, new forms of life developed. Such forms live and grow with the energy provided by hydrogen sulfide. Among these life forms are the tube worms–long, white, worm-like creatures that stand upright, have red tops, and look like tubes of lipstick! They have no eyes, no mouth, and no way to travel. They just seem to stand there on the bottom of the ocean.

2 **Based on the facts in this selection, something that you would NOT expect a tube worm to do is**

 A   live at the bottom of the ocean

 B   swim after insects to feed itself

 C   live on energy from hydrogen sulfide

 D   stand up

NOTICE: Photocopying any part of this book is forbidden by law.

Selection 3

In 1991, hikers in the Alps near the Italian-Austrian border discovered the body of a man frozen in the snow. At first they thought it might be an unfortunate hiker who was caught in a storm. But when the police examined the body and the tools found with it, they were amazed. The metal blade of the man's ax was lashed to a wooden handle with strips of leather. This was not the ax of a modern-day hiker.

Soon an archeologist, a scientist who studies past cultures, was called in. He examined the ax and noted it was made of copper. The frozen man had also carried a knife-blade made of chipped stone. The man was dressed in deerskin clothing and leather boots lined with grass. He carried a six-foot bow for hunting game, and a pouch containing a bone needle, flint, sulfur, and rough tools for starting fires.

3A   **Based on the passage, the body was probably**

     A   a skier of 100 years ago

     B   a hunter of several thousand years ago

     C   a hiker who had disappeared the year before

     D   a hunter of 500 years ago

3B   **Which statement does NOT support your answer to question 3A?**

     A   The police examined the body and found tools.

     B   The ax blade was copper and bound with strips of leather.

     C   The knife-blade was made of chipped stone.

     D   The man's pouch had primitive tools for starting a fire.

NOTICE: Photocopying any part of this book is forbidden by law.

8 IDENTIFYING THE MAIN IDEA AND SUPPORTING DETAILS

MAIN IDEA

GETTING THE IDEA

The test has several questions that ask you what a passage is mostly about. To answer this type of question, you have to identify the passage's **main idea**.

In nonfiction, the main idea is the major or important idea about a topic. It sums up in one sentence what the small pieces of information tell about that topic. Sometimes the main idea is clearly stated in a sentence in a selection. Often, however, the main idea is not directly stated.

In fiction, the main idea may be about the central character in a story, a problem and how it is resolved, or what lesson is learned. The main idea is not usually directly stated. However, it is often expressed in the title of the story.

Read this example.

One of the fascinating details found high up on some old buildings is the gargoyle. A gargoyle is a strange and ugly human or animal figure that decorates the rain gutter of a building. Originally, the word *gargoyle* meant a rainspout. This was a purely practical device that allowed the rainwater to fall free of a building and kept it from damaging the building's stonework. But some stone carver with imagination couldn't just leave it plain. He decided to decorate the spout with an unusual animal head or an evil-looking face. Even when lead pipe drains were invented in the sixteenth century, the strange gargoyle remained, now just a decoration.

What is this passage mostly about?

A   the work of stone carvers

B   lead pipes

C   gargoyles on buildings

D   preventing water from damaging buildings

NOTICE: Photocopying any part of this book is forbidden by law.

Other types of main idea questions will look like the following:

- What is the **main idea** of the selection?
- What is the **best title** for this story?
- This selection **mainly describes** _____.
- This selection is **mainly about** _____.

Read the steps below. They explain what you can do to answer main idea questions, including the passage in the box.

1. **Read the question and underline the key words**. Key words for main idea questions are *mostly about*, *mainly about*, *mainly describes*, *main idea*, and *best title*. **Read the answer choices**. Try to keep these choices in mind as you read the selection.

2. **Read the selection**. After reading, ask yourself, "What was this selection about?" Form your own main idea sentence. The selection in the box on page 60 is about the unusual carvings known as gargoyles.

3. **Reread the question and answer choices**. Look for an answer choice that is similar to your own. If you are not sure of the main idea, look back to the selection once more to see what most of the sentences are about. The correct answer for the passage is Choice **C**.

Use these steps to do the next three examples.

Example 1

     Boats can be made from many different materials such as wood or fiberglass, or, believe it or not, even cement! Building a cement boat is not difficult. People can buy plans that show them how to build a frame for a cement boat. You start with chicken wire and steel bars. Next, force the cement through the chicken wire and allow to harden. Once you place a cement boat in the water, it can remain there safely for many years.

1   **This paragraph is mainly about**

    A   different kinds of boats

    B   building a cement boat

    C   why you use chicken wire and steel bars for a cement boat

    D   why wood boats are not as strong as cement boats

The correct answer is Choice **B**. Most of the sentences explain how to build a cement boat.

Example 2

Mr. Samson was puzzled. It was the third time in a month that an apartment in the building had been robbed, and this time it was his. There were only two doors into the building. Both doors and all ground floor windows were wired with alarms; and besides, there were no signs of forced entry.

"I don't understand it," said Joseph, the security guard. "Both doors have video cameras. From my office, I can watch both entrances on monitors. No one can enter or leave the building without my seeing him."

2   **What is this story mainly about?**

     A   how Joseph works as a security guard

     B   what was taken from Mr. Samson's apartment

     C   how the police investigates a robbery

     D   the question of how a robber entered a building

Remember, in fiction, ask yourself, "Who is this story about? What is the character's problem?" In this selection, Mr. Samson is the main character, and he doesn't understand how robbers got into his apartment. The best answer is Choice **D**.

Example 3

It might be hard to believe, but the tomato and the potato were unknown in Europe before the 1500s. When Columbus returned to Spain from the Western Hemisphere, he brought these plants and many others with him. The new crops were welcomed. They grew very well in Europe and soon became part of the regular diets of the people there. The increased food supplies meant the populations of Europe, Asia, and Africa increased, too.

3   **This selection mainly describes**

     A   what happened when the tomato and the potato were introduced in Europe

     B   when the population of Europe, Asia, and Africa grew

     C   how Columbus discovered the tomato and the potato

     D   the many crops that grew in Europe

 Your teacher will discuss your answer.

NOTICE: Photocopying any part of this book is forbidden by law.

SUPPORTING DETAILS

Beside the main idea, there are **details** that develop the main idea. Details describe or explain a main idea.

A test question about supporting details in a passage usually states the main idea first, then asks the question. Here are two examples: "Which detail supports this main idea?" "Which detail does NOT support this main idea?"

Example 4

Years ago kids in the city played a variety of sidewalk games. Stickball, played with an old broomstick and a pink rubber ball, was a great favorite. Other games played with the same kind of ball were box ball and stoop ball.

Girls, and sometimes boys, played hopscotch. They drew a diagram on the sidewalk with chalk, used a stone for a marker (known as a *potsy*) and hopped the diagram according to local rules. These games were fun and helped pass the time. However, kids rarely play these sidewalk games today.

4　**The main idea of this selection is that years ago city kids played various sidewalk games. Which detail below does NOT support this main idea?**

A　Stickball was a great favorite.

B　Other games played with a ball were box ball and stoop ball.

C　Kids rarely play sidewalk games today.

D　Girls, and sometimes boys, played hopscotch.

Answer Choices A, B, and D all give details about sidewalk games. The correct choice is **C**. It is the only detail that does not support the main idea.

NOTICE: Photocopying any part of this book is forbidden by law.

63

USING A WEB TO UNDERSTAND MAIN IDEA AND SUPPORTING DETAILS

Webs can help you see more clearly the connection between a main idea and its details. When you see a web on the test, be sure to read it carefully, so that you know how to complete it.

In a main idea web, the middle circle or box states the main idea in a sentence or a phrase. The outer circles or boxes provide details about this main idea. This kind of web is used in the next example.

Example 5

Dogs have been useful to humans for thousands of years. Throughout history dogs have been used for hunting—to track animals, to retrieve birds, or to chase foxes. Some dogs have been trained to herd sheep and cattle. Others have been used to guide the blind. Still others have guarded homes or businesses, while others have simply been loyal and loving friends and companions.

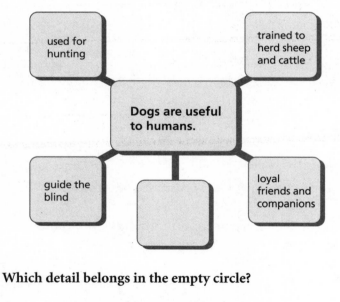

5   **Which detail belongs in the empty circle?**

    A   used to guard homes and businesses

    B   used as pets

    C   play with cats

    D   are housebroken

Choice **A** is correct. Choices C and D do not support the main idea. Choice B has already been said in other words, "loyal friends and companions."

NOTICE: Photocopying any part of this book is forbidden by law.

TIPS AND STRATEGIES FOR IDENTIFYING THE MAIN IDEA AND SUPPORTING DETAILS

☞ Remember that the **main idea** is what a selection is mostly about.

☞ To identify the main idea:

- Read the question first and underline the key words. Key words for main idea questions are *mostly about*, *mainly about*, *mainly describes*, *main idea*, and *best title*. Read the answer choices. Try to keep these choices in mind as you read the selection.

- Read the selection. After reading, ask yourself, "What was this selection about?" Form your own main idea statement.

- Reread the question and answer choices. Look for an answer choice that is similar to your own. If you are not sure of the main idea, look back to the selection once more. In nonfiction, decide what most of the sentences are about. In fiction, look for the main character and what problem the character faces.

☞ Don't confuse a detail with the main idea. Remember that **supporting details** support the main idea by describing or explaining it. Pay attention to the details to help you understand the main idea.

☞ **Webs** can help you see the connection between a main idea and its details. Remember that usually the middle or larger circle or box contains the main idea.

NOTICE: Photocopying any part of this book is forbidden by law.

SELECTIONS FOR PRACTICE

Selection 1

Are you looking for thrills and chills this winter? Hundreds of vacationers are heading for the wilderness of Yellowstone National Park. There, they will take part in cross-country skiing tours sponsored by park officials and tour companies. In the past, only a few brave souls, most of them park rangers, were allowed to go into Yellowstone's back country in winter. Those who survived told horrible tales of being almost trapped in snow, or nearly freezing to death. Today, modern equipment, trained guides, effective preparation, and detailed maps have reduced the risk. Even people with no wilderness experience can sign up for a tour, provided they can ski and have the strength to spend long days gliding across the snowbound country.

1 **The best title for this selection is**

A   "The Benefits of Cross-Country Skiing"

B   "Touring Yellowstone's Back Country in Winter"

C   "Yellowstone's Trained Guides"

D   "Some Dangers at Yellowstone"

Selection 2

One of the great successes of the twentieth century toy business was the hula-hoop. But this fad, which hit its peak in the 1950s, is really at least three thousand years old. Children in ancient Egypt played with hoops made from dried grapevines. In the 1300s, a craze for "hooping" swept England. Doctors credited the fad with causing back problems and heart attacks.

In 1957, two California toy manufacturers, Arthur Melin and Richard Knerr, took a trip to Australia, where they saw bamboo exercise rings. When the men returned home, they began making plastic hoops in bright colors; and the hula hoop was born. The fad caught on! The company sold more than 100 million hoops in the first six months on the market. The craze spread around the world and made Melin and Knerr very rich.

    NOTICE: Photocopying any part of this book is forbidden by law.

2 **The selection is mainly about**

    A   the twentieth-century toy business

    B   Arthur Melin and Richard Knerr

    C   the history of the hula hoop

    D   how to market an invention

Selection 3

The name that defined rock n' roll in the mid-1950s was Elvis Presley. Presley was born in 1935 in Tupelo, Mississippi; but he moved to Memphis, Tennessee, when he was thirteen. His first success was the recording of "That's All Right, Mama," a blues song written by African American singer Arthur Crudup. It won him a recording contract with RCA Victor.

At that time, black music was just starting to be marketed to white audiences. Through national promotion, Presley's next releases—"Heartbreak Hotel" and "Hound Dog"—became overnight hits. Presley combined a driving vocal style with a fast, rhythmic, country-and-western instrumental sound. That style, along with his sideburns and stage personality, made him a favorite of teen fans and the first rock n' roll superstar.

3 **The main idea of this selection is how Elvis Presley became a rock n' roll superstar. Which detail does NOT support this main idea?**

    A   Elvis was born in Tupelo, Mississippi.

    B   "Heartbreak Hotel" was an overnight hit.

    C   "That's All Right, Mama" won him a recording contract.

    D   Teen fans loved his sideburns and stage personality.

NOTICE: Photocopying any part of this book is forbidden by law.

Selection 4

A football quarterback must have an amazing collection of skills. First of all, he must be able to make split-second decisions under pressure. He must be able to judge what is happening downfield, decide where to pass or run, and do this when strong, determined opponents are hurtling at him. He must be able to throw accurately, run with speed and agility, and change plays at the last moment.

A football quarterback must also play day after day, despite injuries that would leave the average person in pain and agony. Football is a tough game with a lot of physical contact, Much of a team's effort is aimed at bringing down the other team's quarterback. Few quarterbacks have escaped knee and shoulder injuries, twisted ankles, broken ribs, and so on—yet they love playing the game.

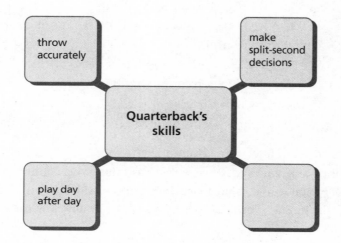

4   **Look at the web. What detail belongs in the empty box?**

A   be big

B   act defensively

C   run with speed

D   get injured

   NOTICE: Photocopying any part of this book is forbidden by law.

9 ANALYZING STORY ELEMENTS

On the test you will find a variety of questions about **story elements**. These elements are:

character: the people or animals in the story

setting: where and when the story takes place. Authors don't always tell you directly. You have to use clues in the story to help you figure the setting out.

plot: the events in the story. Plots usually include a problem, efforts to solve it, and a resolution.

theme: the most important idea in the story. Sometimes it's a lesson, and sometimes it's an insight that a character gains.

CHARACTER

Every story has characters. They might be people, animals, or other kinds of beings. Some stories have only one **main character**. But many stories have more than one.

The author provides the most details about the main character. The main character usually has the problem that must be solved.

NOTICE: Photocopying any part of this book is forbidden by law.

Here is an example of a test question about the main character.

Example 1

"Hey, Andy, are you ready for tonight?" Joey said, poking Andy playfully in the ribs.

"Oh, hi, Joey!" Andy laughed nervously. Joey, Leon, and Daryl had invited him to join their club. All Andy had to do was knock on the door of an old deserted house at night.

Leon grinned at him. "Hey, you are going to be just fine! And when this is done, you will be one of us, man!"

Andy wasn't so sure. Yes, he'd wanted to be friends with these guys ever since he had moved to Northport. But now that he'd been invited to join the club, he wasn't sure he wanted to. Knocking on the door of a deserted house sounded silly. And what might be lurking around the deserted house? Andy didn't want the chance to find out.

1 **Who is the most important character in this story?**

A   Daryl

B   Leon

C   Joey

D   Andy

Choice **D** is correct. All of the choices are characters in the story, but Andy is the most important character. You can telll this because you see the action through his eyes. You learn the most about Andy's feelings.

A character might act *brave*, *funny*, *lazy*, *kind*, *happy*, or even *mysterious*. Authors may use these adjectives to describe a character. However, authors don't always describe a character directly. You must determine this yourself. Here is how you can answer a test question about what a character is like: **Pay attention to what a character says or thinks and the way the character acts**.

   NOTICE: Photocopying any part of this book is forbidden by law.

The next example asks you to figure out how a character feels.

Example 2

"Listen, Jassy, I don't know about this," Annie hung back, two steps behind her friend.

"Come on, Annie. Mrs. Fletcher isn't so bad. You'll see." Jassy started up the steps of the tumbled-down porch.

"But she's always been so mean," Annie objected. "She's always yelled at us." Annnie followed Jassy up the steps anyway.

"Look, Jassy explained, "my Mom said that Mrs. Fletcher needs help. She's not going to bite you!"

2 **From this passage, you can guess that Annie is**

    A   happy

    B   unwilling to help

    C   hesitant

    D   angry

Choice **C** is correct. You know this through the way Annie acts—she hangs back. She doesn't want to go with Jassy, but she doesn't refuse. She follows her friend, so she is not unwilling, but she is *hesitant*.

COMPARING CHARACTERS

Sometimes a test question asks you to compare and contrast one character with another. Remember that when you **compare**, you see in what way or ways the characters are **alike**. When you **contrast**, you see in what way or ways the characters are **different**.

Here is an example that asks you to compare and contrast characters.

Example 3

Jodie and Jill were identical twins. I never met two girls who looked more alike. Both had the same dark, wavy hair and bright, dark eyes. However, they were as different as sunshine and shade. Jodie was cheerful and outgoing, quick with a joke and always laughing. Jill was reserved and quiet. She never wanted the spotlight, and always let Jodie do the talking. But I knew if I wanted a friend who would stand by me in a crisis, it was Jill for sure.

3A   **In what way were Jodie and Jill alike?**

A   Both loved to tell jokes.

B   Both were quiet and reserved.

C   They looked identical.

D   Both were outgoing.

Choice **C** is the correct answer. The selection tells you directly that they looked exactly alike.

3B   **How was Jill different from Jodie?**

A   Jill was more outgoing.

B   Jill was shorter.

C   Jill was older.

D   Jill was quieter.

Choice **D** is the correct answer. The selection doesn't tell anything about their height. Since they were twins, they were the same age. Jodie was described as outgoing, while Jill was reserved.

   NOTICE: Photocopying any part of this book is forbidden by law.

USING A DIAGRAM TO COMPARE AND CONTRAST CHARACTERS

A **Venn diagram** can help you to organize the ways in which two characters are alike and different. The headings on the diagram name the characters. Details about each character are written in the circles. The outer circles indicate the differences. The inner circle shows the similarities.

A test question might ask you to add a missing detail to a diagram.

Example 4

Field Andrews and Jason McCabe had been partners for twenty years. Both were wise businessmen. Both had a "nose" for a good deal. Andrews, the senior partner, was the idea man. He was the one who dreamed up the inventions.

McCabe, the junior partner, didn't have too many original ideas, but he was one smooth-talking salesman. Why, he could charm the stripes off a skunk! So he was the one who talked all the big money men into supporting projects. Before they knew what had hit them, those rich fellows were signing their names to big checks. Together, the two partners made Andrews & McCabe a huge success.

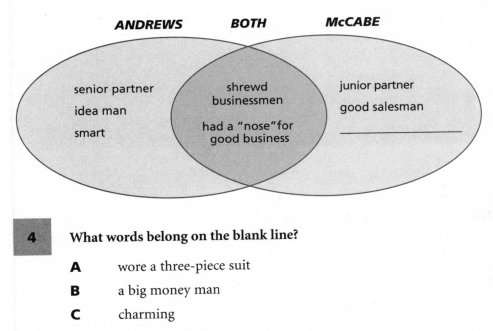

ANDREWS	BOTH	McCABE
senior partner	shrewd businessmen	junior partner
idea man		good salesman
smart	had a "nose" for good business	_____

4   **What words belong on the blank line?**

    A   wore a three-piece suit

    B   a big money man

    C   charming

    D   older than Andrews

Choice **C** is correct. Information from the selection states that McCabe could charm the stripes off a skunk. The other information is either not stated or refers to Andrews.

NOTICE: Photocopying any part of this book is forbidden by law.

SETTING

The **setting** of a story is **where** and **when** the story events take place. Authors don't always name the place and time of a story. But you can look for word clues in the story that suggest the place and time.

Test questions about setting might look like the ones in the example below.

Example 5

Tom straightened up and stretched his aching back. He glanced at the sun. It was a good time to stop and eat the corn bread and molasses Ma had packed for him. It was still only mid-April, but the sun was already hot, already warming the soil beneath his bare feet. Since dawn, he'd been planting potatoes on the two acres behind their Indiana cabin. Pa, he knew, was busy plowing the field across the road with Old Charlie, their mule. As Tom ate, he wondered if Pa would let him come along when he drove the wagon to town tomorrow.

5A   **Where does Tom live?**

    A   in a small town in Indiana

    B   in a large city in Indiana

    C   on a farm in Indiana

    D   across the road from Old Charlie

Choice **C** is correct. The author tells you that Tom is in Indiana. Tom's planting and his father's plowing are clues that they live on a farm.

5B   **When does this story most likely take place?**

    A   late evening

    B   dawn

    C   late morning

    D   early evening

Choice **C** is correct. The sun is out and hot, so it's not in the evening. Late morning is the only answer that makes sense.

NOTICE: Photocopying any part of this book is forbidden by law.

PLOT

The order of important events from the beginning to the end of a story is called the story **plot**. A story plot usually focuses on two elements: a main character who has a **problem** and what the character does to solve the problem. The way the character solves the problem is called the **solution**, or **resolution**.

Read the next example, and follow the plot closely.

Example 6

Once there was a crow that was almost dying of thirst. At last it came upon a pitcher that contained some water. But alas! The water level in the pitcher was so low that the poor crow could not reach the water to drink it.

The crow finally thought of what to do. He flew off and came back with a pebble in its beak and dropped it into the pitcher. Then he got another pebble and did the same thing. Over and over the crow dropped pebbles into the pitcher. With each pebble, the water level rose a little. At last the water level was high enough for the thirsty crow to drink.

6A **What was the crow's problem?**

A He could not reach the water in the pitcher.

B The water was not fresh.

C The pitcher was empty.

D He couldn't find water.

Choice **A** is correct. The last sentence in the first paragraph tells us this.

6B **How was the problem resolved?**

A The crow looked somewhere else for water.

B The crow gave up and did not find water.

C The crow broke the pitcher to get the water.

D The crow dropped pebbles into the pitcher to raise the water level.

Choice **D** is correct. In the second paragraph you read that the crow dropped pebbles into the pitcher.

NOTICE: Photocopying any part of this book is forbidden by law.

THEME

An author often has an important idea, message, or lesson to tell readers. This is called the **theme**. The theme might be about the importance of kindness, never giving up, the value of friendship, and so on.

Authors don't usually state a theme directly in a story. You must figure it out from what happens to the characters. Some types of stories, such as fables, *do* state the theme directly as a moral, or lesson. Here are some examples of how themes can be stated:

> Old friends are the best friends.
> Laughter is the best medicine of all.
> Don't count your chickens before they hatch.
> Honesty is the best policy.

Read the example below.

Example 7

One hot summer day a fox was strolling through an orchard. He came upon a grapevine trained on a trellis and saw a fat bunch of grapes ripening just overhead.

"Just the thing to quench my thirst," he said. He drew back a bit, took a running start and jumped for the grapes. But he missed! Turning round again he jumped a second time, but still could not reach those grapes. Again and again he tried, but they were out of reach.

At last the fox gave up. As he walked away, he muttered, "Oh, those grapes are probably sour, anyway!"

7 **Which sentence best states the theme?**

A Honesty is the best policy.

B It is easy to criticize what you can't have.

C Look before you leap.

D You can't please everyone.

Choice **B** is correct. The fox wanted the grapes and couldn't get them. But instead of admitting they were beyond his reach, he pretended they weren't worth having.

 NOTICE: Photocopying any part of this book is forbidden by law.

TIPS AND STRATEGIES
FOR ANALYZING STORY ELEMENTS

☞ A **main character** in a story is the most important character. To understand what a character is like:

- Look for words that describe the character.

- Pay attention to what a character says and does.

☞ Two characters in a story may be **alike** in some ways and **different** in others. Pay attention to authors' descriptions of characters. Watch how the characters act, and what other characters say about them. Look for clue words that signal whether an author is comparing or contrasting characters.

☞ **Diagrams** can help you compare and contrast characters in a quick, easy way.

☞ The **setting** of a story is **where** and **when** it takes place. You may find that your own experience and what you know about the world will help you figure out the setting. Be sure to do the following:

- Look for words that describe a place.

- Pay attention to other clue words about the land, water, and weather, as well as other details about a place.

- Pay attention to clue words about time such as time of day, season, year, and so on.

- A story may be set in the past, in the present, or in the future.

☞ The **plot** of a story is what happens. The plot often centers around a main character who has a problem and tries to get it solved. Pay attention to the **events** in the story.

☞ The **theme** of a story is the author's message about an important idea or lesson in life. Author's don't usually tell you the theme directly. You need to figure it out. To identify the theme, ask yourself:

- "What lesson did the character learn?" or

- "What does the author want me to know about _____?"

NOTICE: Photocopying any part of this book is forbidden by law.

SELECTIONS FOR PRACTICE

Selection 1

Terri and I sat facing each other on the train. The next stop was *his* town. Jimmy was my new crush—the most gorgeous guy I'd ever seen! I was getting a stomachache. I just knew I wouldn't know what to say!

"Janey? What will you do when we go in?" asked Terri.

I stared at her. "*Go in*?"

"Yes, as in 'go into the store.' You do want to go in to the store where he works?"

"Well, sure," I gulped. I hadn't thought about this part.

"So, what will you say? Are you going to ask for him?"

"Ask for him?" I dropped my voice to a whisper. "Who? Jimmy?"

"No, Elvis. Who else are we going to find?"

"Terri! I can't ask for *him*!"

"Well, it would be easier to get information if you just ask," said Terri reasonably.

1A   **Which phrase best describes Janey, the narrator?**

   A   bold and brave

   B   carefree and silly

   C   nervous and excited

   D   reasonable and calm

1B   **How does Terri differ from Janey?**

   A   Terri is older.

   B   Terri is calm and matter-of-fact.

   C   Terri is very excited and nervous.

   D   Terri isn't interested in where they are going.

NOTICE: Photocopying any part of this book is forbidden by law.

Selection 2

Marge and Teesha had been friends since second grade. They both wore their hair in ponytails until the eighth grade; then both got their hair cut short the same day. Both were passionate about ballet, and neither one could stand pizza. But Marge came from a big family—four brothers and four sisters, while Teesha had just one younger sister.

Maybe because Marge was the youngest and used to being the baby, she was a little spoiled. Although the girls were the same age, Teesha seemed older, more mature. She was used to being in charge of her little sister.

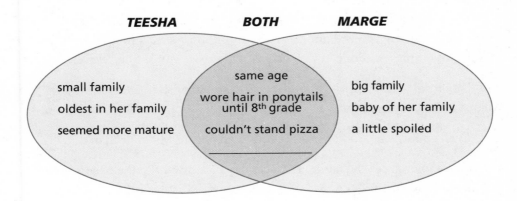

TEESHA   **BOTH**   **MARGE**

small family

oldest in her family

seemed more mature

same age

wore hair in ponytails until 8th grade

couldn't stand pizza

big family

baby of her family

a little spoiled

2   **The diagram compares the two characters. Which detail belongs on the blank line?**

    A   had four brothers and four sisters

    B   used to being in charge

    C   loved ballet

    D   youngest in family

NOTICE: Photocopying any part of this book is forbidden by law.

Selection 3

Long ago, when Anansi was just a young spider, he lived in the kingdom of a powerful chief. One day the chief decided his daughter should marry. "Whoever guesses my secret name shall be my husband," said the daughter. The chief agreed with the plan, and so the contest was announced.

Now Anansi wanted to marry the beautiful princess, and he knew what to do. That evening, he crawled onto the roof of the daughter's hut. She was talking with her friends. He let himself down on a thread and listened. He learned that the daughter's secret name was Kiri the Beautiful.

Anansi was happy. He would win the princess and inherit the kingdom! When he got home he began to brag about it to his friends. But Lizard said to him, "Anansi, surely you will not go yourself. You must send a messenger instead. It is the way things are done in rich houses. Otherwise you get no respect."

"Is that so?" said Anansi. "But messengers are expensive." Everyone knew Anansi hated to spend money.

"I will go for you," said Lizard. "I require no reward but your thanks."

Anansi told Lizard the name. The next day Lizard went to the chief's house. "I have come to claim the princess! Her name is Kiri the Beautiful!"

"He is indeed clever," said Kiri. "All right. I will marry him."

The next day, the wedding procession passed by Anansi's hut while he was waiting for an invitation to come claim his bride. He saw that Lizard was seated next to the princess and was wearing a crown! He was married to the princess.

"That sneaky Lizard tricked me!" shouted Anansi. "He had better watch out for me. Next time I see him I will chop off his head!"

To this day, Lizard stretches his neck this way and that. He is watching out for Anansi.

NOTICE: Photocopying any part of this book is forbidden by law.

3A   **What is the setting of this story?**

A   a modern city

B   200 years into the future

C   pioneer days on the American frontier

D   a make-believe kingdom long ago

3B   **What is the problem in this story?**

A   The princess does not want to marry.

B   Anansi is fighting for his life.

C   A Lizard hurt his neck.

D   Anansi wants to marry the princess.

3C   **What is Anansi's mistake?**

A   He eavesdropped on the princess.

B   He tells Lizard the secret name.

C   He insults the chief.

D   He has a bad temper.

3D   **Which sentence best states the theme of the story?**

A   True love never runs smooth.

B   One good turn deserves another.

C   Everyone needs friends.

D   Be careful of whom you trust.

10 ANALYZING NONFICTION ELEMENTS

Nonfiction is about real people, places, events, and things. A few examples of nonfiction are biographies, information articles, how-to manuals, interviews, and newspaper stories. These kinds of texts are **sources of information**.

On a test, questions about nonfiction might look like some of the following:

- What kind of information is given in this passage?

- In which source would you find this kind of information?

- What kind of information might you expect to find in a book entitled *The Ancient Egyptians*?

- The best title for this chapter would be _____.

- Which newspaper headline would indicate a story about a space mission?

- Why is the word *never* in italics in the passage?

The steps you have been using to answer questions in other lessons will also help you answer questions about the elements of nonfiction.

DIFFERENT KINDS OF NONFICTION TEXTS

You can usually identify the type of nonfiction after reading a small part of it. For example, you know that a **biography** is a true story about a person's life written by another person. You know that an **information article** presents facts about a topic. You know that a **how-to** text contains directions on how to make or do something.

Read the examples on the next page and answer the questions.

Example 1

Heat the garlic in oil until lightly golden. Add diced tomatoes, cover, and cook for 20 minutes over a low heat until the tomatoes are tender. Crumble the tuna into small pieces and add to the tomato mixture. Add a quarter cup of sliced black olives. Simmer just enough to warm the tuna through; you don't want to boil it. Transfer cooked spaghetti to a serving bowl and pour the tomato and tuna mixture over it. Add parsley, salt, and pepper to taste.

1 **In what kind of source would you most likely find this passage?**

A a health textbook

B a biography of a famous chef

C a cookbook

D an encyclopedia of foods around the world

While you might fight a recipe in the sources named in Choices B and D, a cookbook is the most likely source for cooking directions. The correct answer is Choice **C**.

Example 2

HARRISON LAND TO BECOME PARK

Belle Ridge, NJ—Town officials announced today that the 180-acre estate belonging to the late Jacob Richard Harrison will become a town park and wildlife preserve. The estate, which has been in the Harrison family since 1753, was left to the town in Harrison's will. The land includes a lake, a wetlands, wooded areas, and meadows. Town officials plan to keep most of it in a natural state and to allow hiking.

2 **This selection would probably be found in**

A a nature magazine

B a newspaper

C an animal encyclopedia

D a brochure about wooded areas of New Jersey

Choice **B** is correct. This is a report of a recent event. The word *today* gives you a clue. The headline and the writing form also tell you this selection would most likely be found in a newspaper.

NOTICE: Photocopying any part of this book is forbidden by law.

In following example you will answer a question about the information itself.

Example 3

BASIC RULES FOR COMPUTER CROSSWORD

Objective:

To be the player with the highest score by forming crosswords with the highest possible letter values.

To Begin:

Each player starts with seven letters. The first player makes a word using two or more letters and places them on the board.

3   **Why would this passage be in a computer-game manual?**

    A   It presents the history of a computer game.

    B   It explains how to play a computer game.

    C   It tries to appeal to game players.

    D   It offers updated rules for an old game.

Choice **B** is the correct answer. The writing form is instructions. A manual is a book of instructions that is included with a particular product.

CHAPTER TITLES AND HEADINGS

Chapter titles and headings help to organize information. They let you know what you are going to read about. A **chapter title** tells you about the most important topic or topics in that chapter. A **heading** or **subheading** in a chapter tells you what kind of information you will read in a particular section.

Think about a chapter title and subheading for the sample questions on the next page.

    NOTICE: Photocopying any part of this book is forbidden by law.

Example 4

4 | In a biography of Abraham Lincoln, which chapter would most likely have information about his boyhood?

A A Backwoods Boy

B A Country Lawyer

C Lincoln and Slavery

D The Dreadful War

 Your teacher will discuss your answer.

Example 5

The best place for a chicken coop is on a hill or on a slope where water does not collect when it rains. Avoid low spots. Puddles and muddy ground can cause chickens to get sick.

The more room your chickens have, the happier they will be. A coop 8 feet by 12 feet is big enough for thirty regular-size chickens. Be sure the roof is high enough for you to stand up inside when you clean the coop.

5 | The title of the chapter from which this passage was taken is "A Home for Your Chickens." Which would be the best subheading for this section of the chapter?

A Treating Sick Chickens

B Coop Location and Design

C Nests

D Cleaning the Coop

Choice **B** is the correct answer. The main focus in the passage is on where to put the coop and how big to make it.

NOTICE: Photocopying any part of this book is forbidden by law.

A newspaper headline is another kind of title. It grabs readers' attention and sums up what a news story is about.

Example 6

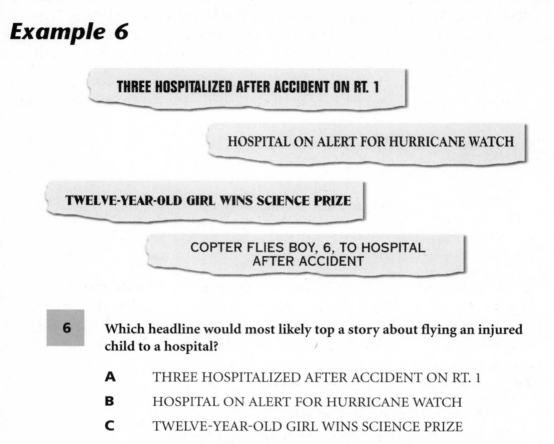

THREE HOSPITALIZED AFTER ACCIDENT ON RT. 1

HOSPITAL ON ALERT FOR HURRICANE WATCH

TWELVE-YEAR-OLD GIRL WINS SCIENCE PRIZE

COPTER FLIES BOY, 6, TO HOSPITAL AFTER ACCIDENT

6 Which headline would most likely top a story about flying an injured child to a hospital?

A THREE HOSPITALIZED AFTER ACCIDENT ON RT. 1

B HOSPITAL ON ALERT FOR HURRICANE WATCH

C TWELVE-YEAR-OLD GIRL WINS SCIENCE PRIZE

D COPTER FLIES BOY, 6, TO HOSPITAL AFTER ACCIDENT

Choice **D** is the correct answer. Only this headline mentions both a helicopter and a child.

NOTICE: Photocopying any part of this book is forbidden by law.

UNDERSTANDING SPECIAL PRINT

Writers sometimes put certain words in **dark print**, called **boldface**, or in *slanted type*, called *italics*. The words appear in special print to get your attention. The words in bold or italic print may be important **topic words** and **terms** that are defined. Or, they may be **key words** such as *not, always, before,* and *after,* used to make sure that you clearly understand a statement or direction.

As you read the next example, think about the reason for the words in special print.

Example 7

One of the greatest developments in the history of chocolate came in the nineteenth century. The Swiss invented a process called **conching**, by which chocolate is kneaded into a smooth and velvety texture. This was a great improvement over the coarsely grained chocolate people ate.

To use chocolate for homemade desserts, grate semisweet chocolate squares as finely as possible. Put them in the top part of a double boiler. Melt extremely slowly *over* hot water, not *in* it.

7A **Why is the word *conching* in boldface?**

A because it is a brand name

B to identify a special term used in making chocolate

C to warn you against saying it

D to suggest that readers look up the word in a dictionary

Choice **B** is the correct answer. It is a special term that describes part of the chocolate-making process.

7B **Why is the word *over* in italics?**

A to show readers this step does not matter

B to indicate it is a difficult word

C to show which step comes next in cooking chocolate

D to stress that it's important for the chocolate to be melted over water

Choice **D** is correct. Recipes can go wrong if not followed carefully.

NOTICE: Photocopying any part of this book is forbidden by law.

APPLYING PICTURES TO TEXTS

When a selection has **pictures**, study them to see what information they explain or support. Nonfiction selections often have photographs; but they also might have illustrations.

Sometimes the test will ask you to choose a picture instead of a sentence as your answer. The correct picture is the one closest to a description of something you read.

Example 8

       Rambling Roses—the kind that will grow up walls and along trellises— can grow to great heights. One old rose grew 25 feet high as it wrapped itself around a holly tree. Roses started out as wild plants. Now there are often two varieties of the same rose: the wild version and its domesticated cousin. The wild Burnet Rose still rambles across the Scottish moors. Its cousin, the Scotch Briar, can be found in gardens across Britain.

8   **The illustration above shows a Scotch Briar rose that**

    A   has one gigantic bloom on each branch

    B   has leaves shaped like needles

    C   grows straight up towards the sky

    D   has clusters of flowers growing along each branch.

The correct answer is **D**. The illustration shows a rose with many flowers on its branches. For this reason, choice A must be incorrect. The branches hang down, so choice C is incorrect. And we can see that the leaves do not look like needles, so choice B is also incorrect.

NOTICE: Photocopying any part of this book is forbidden by law.

APPLYING DIAGRAMS TO TEXTS

Diagrams are special kinds of pictures with labels. A diagram might show the parts of something, or how something works. A diagram might illustrate how to make or repair something. A diagram might also show how to play a game or a sport.

The test might ask a question about a diagram that supports a passage. Read the example that follows.

Example 9

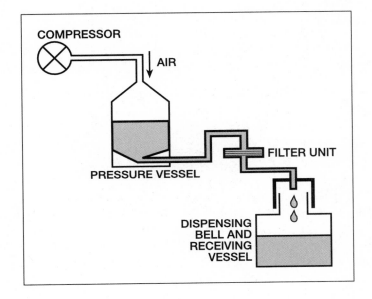

9 The diagram shows a filter system. It shows liquid passing through a filter unit. Where was this liquid right before it entered the filter?

A in the compressor

B in the dispensing bell

C in the pressure vessel

D in the receiving vessel

 Your teacher will discuss your answer.

NOTICE: Photocopying any part of this book is forbidden by law.

TIPS AND STRATEGIES
FOR ANALYZING NONFICTION ELEMENTS

☞ Remember that **nonfiction** deals with **real** people, places, events, and things. There are different kinds of nonfiction texts, but all are sources of information.

☞ Book titles, chapter titles, and headings help to organize information. They let you know what you are going to read about. Read them carefully.

- A **book title** gives you an idea of the main topic.

- A **chapter title** tells you about the most important topic or topics in that chapter.

- A **heading** or **subheading** in a chapter tells you what kind of information is in a particular section.

- A **newspaper headline** grabs your attention and offers the most important idea in the news story.

☞ Some key words and terms are often put in **boldface** or *italics*. Make sure you recognize why they are in a special print.

☞ Look carefully at **pictures** and **diagrams** when they are included. They help you better understand information in the texts. Be sure you know what facts the pictures or diagrams explain.

NOTICE: Photocopying any part of this book is forbidden by law.

SELECTIONS FOR PRACTICE

Selection 1

Long ago, the first rough standards of measurement were based on the human body. A storekeeper might use his own hand as a measure and sell his salt by the handful. He could figure out his profit accurately because he had already measured the number of handfuls in his bags when filling them. The measure of a foot was originally the length of a man's foot. The yard was originally the length of his walking pace.

In the Middle Ages, if a disagreement arose about the length, width, or height of something, the sheriff would go to the church door and take the first twelve men who came out. He would make them stand in a line with the toe of one man's foot touching the heel of the man in front. The length of the men's twelve feet was taken and averaged. It made a good standard of measurement, which was then used to settle the disagreement.

A uniform standard came only gradually. Our word *mile* comes from the Romans; it meant "a thousand paces." But there are several different miles still in use. There is our statute mile (5,280 feet); but the Dutch mile is several yards shorter. The Danish mile is equal to four and a half statute miles. A mile on land is different than a mile at sea, too.

1A **In which source would you most likely find this selection?**

    A   in a newspaper's editorial page

    B   in a book about the history of measurement

    C   in a textbook about the Middle Ages

    D   in a biography

1B **In which of the following chapters would you expect to find the above information?**

    A   Old Ways of Travel

    B   Settling Disputes

    C   Measuring Sand

    D   Weights and Measures of the Past

NOTICE: Photocopying any part of this book is forbidden by law.

Selection 2

Lacrosse is a team sport that originated in contests among various Native American groups in North America. In the game, players use a netted stick, the **crosse**, to throw or bat a ball into a goal. Players may also kick the ball into the goal. The rules were first written down in 1867 by Dr. George Beers, a native of Montreal. The game spread to other English-speaking countries.

2 **Why is the word *crosse* in boldface print?**

A   to help the reader pronounce it

B   to make the reader look it up in a dictionary

C   to explain the popularity of the game

D   to call attention to a special term, and its nearby definition

Selection 3

Hedge trimmers are designed to shape shrubs and hedges. Occasionally, a twig or branch will get caught in the trimmer's teeth. To unjam the blades, *first unplug the trimmer* and lay it on a flat surface. Hold the handle of the trimmer to steady it, and use a stick to push out the blockage. Don't use a screwdriver or other metal tool which may damage the blades.

3 **Why are the words *first unplug the trimmer* in italics?**

A   to help the reader pronounce them

B   to show how the trimmer works

C   to stress that this step is very important

D   to call attention to a special term

NOTICE: Photocopying any part of this book is forbidden by law.

PART 4: EVALUATING AND EXTENDING MEANING

NOTICE: Photocopying any part of this book is forbidden by law.

93

11 MAKING PREDICTIONS ABOUT TEXTS

In your daily life and when reading stories, you no doubt have made guesses about things that might happen. When you make a guess about what might happen, you are **making a prediction**. The prediction is based on what already has happened and your own knowledge and experiences.

You will find questions on the test that ask you to make a prediction. Here is an example of one.

> Nancy looked out the window. It was a beautiful, clear morning, perfect for painting outside. Just yesterday she'd bought herself some new paints, and she was anxious to try them out. She knew of just the spot, too—near the tennis courts in the park. Quickly she gathered her materials. She packed a lunch, and then she headed for the door.

What do you think Nancy will do next?

A   She will play tennis at the tennis courts in the park.

B   She will eat her lunch under a tree in the park.

C   She will take a nap before she goes to the park.

D   She will go to the park near the tennis courts to paint.

Use the following steps to answer the question above as well as other questions that ask you to make predictions. Remember to always read the question and answer choices before you read the selection so you know what is being asked.

1. **Think about the information you get from the selection—the story clues**. Story clues in the passage above are that Nancy thought it was a perfect day to paint, and she had new paints she wanted to try.

2. **Think of what you know from your own life about the way things happen and the way people behave**. You know that before people go somewhere to enjoy a hobby, they usually prepare. They think about where to go, and they gather the things they need.

 NOTICE: Photocopying any part of this book is forbidden by law.

3. **Combine the story clues and what you know about life to make a prediction about what will happen. Reread the question and answer choices. See which answer choice is closest to your prediction.** You can predict that Nancy will go to the park to paint. Choice **D** makes the most sense.

Now read the following examples and answer the questions.

Example 1

"Sue, come on! We're ready to go!" Myra called from downstairs.

"I'll be right there," Sue answered. She knew Myra, Joe, and Josh were waiting for her. But she stayed where she was, in the little bedroom at the top of the stairs. For the tenth time, she looked in the mirror to check her outfit. Was she dressed right, or were her jeans too casual? Would Josh be impressed, or would he be sorry he'd asked her to go out to the movies and dinner?

Now or never, she thought, heading down the stairs. With relief, Sue saw Josh's admiring glance. And she saw that Myra was wearing jeans, too.

"Hey, you look great!" Josh said as they headed toward the car.

1 **What will Sue probably do next?**

   A   She will go back upstairs to change a few more times.

   B   She will go out and enjoy the evening with her friends.

   C   She will decide to call other friends and go out with them.

   D   She will stay home and read a book.

The story clues are that Sue sees Myra is also wearing jeans, and Josh compliments her on her appearance. You know that these kinds of things make people feel good and comfortable among their friends. You can predict that she will go out and enjoy the evening with her friends. Choice **B** makes the most sense.

NOTICE: Photocopying any part of this book is forbidden by law.

Example 2

Mr. and Mrs. Saxon knew they had to mow their lawn today. They wouldn't have time to do it tomorrow before their outdoor party, and they wanted the yard to look perfect. They had saved up for a new power mower and were glad they had one now. They were tired of taking turns using the old push mower! But they had kept the old one, just in case.

2   **Suppose the power mower doesn't work? What will the Saxons probably do?**

    A   They will hire someone to mow the lawn today.

    B   They will mow the lawn the following day.

    C   They will take turns using the old push mower.

    D   They will not mow the lawn until after the party.

The story clues are that the Saxons really want to mow the lawn the day *before* their party and that they had saved up to buy the power mower. After spending money on a power mower, you know that most people would not then go out and hire someone. So the Saxons will probably take turns using the old mower. Answer Choice **C** is correct.

Example 3

Harold was a man of habit. He always set his alarm for 6:30 AM. He got the clothes he would wear the next day ready the night before. He always went to bed by 11 PM. When he awoke he would shower, dress, and eat breakfast—always cereal with a piece of fruit and one cup of coffee.

Harold always bought a newspaper at the corner store, caught the 7:16 train, and arrived at his office at 8:30. He would have another cup of coffee and read his email until 8:45.

3   **Suppose Harold were to decide to work out at a gym. When would you expect him to go to the gym?**

    A   on a different day each week

    B   at the same time and on the same days every week

    C   whenever he felt like it

    D   at 7:30 A.M.

NOTICE: Photocopying any part of this book is forbidden by law.

The story clues reveal that Harold likes to do things on a regular schedule, so Choices A and C can be eliminated right away. At 7:30 AM, he is on a train, so Choice D is not logical. Since Harold is such a man of habit, answer Choice **B** makes the most sense.

TIPS AND STRATEGIES
FOR MAKING PREDICTIONS ABOUT TEXTS

☞ When you **make a prediction**, you make a guess about what might happen.

☞ To make a prediction, use story clues of what has already happened and what you know from your own knowledge and experience.

☞ To answer a prediction question:

- Find the part of the story that has the clues you need to answer the question. Reread this part of the selection.

- Make a prediction of your own. See which answer choice is closest to your prediction.

NOTICE: Photocopying any part of this book is forbidden by law.

SELECTIONS FOR PRACTICE

Selection 1

On Tuesday, Emily walked into her history class to find the teacher passing out a test. "Oh, no! I completely forgot!" thought Emily. Quickly she looked over her notes before Mrs. Lambert told the students to close their notebooks and begin the test.

Emily tried her best, but she knew she hadn't done very well at all. She had somehow let this test escape her mind and hadn't studied for it. "Mrs. Lambert is nice," Emily thought. "Maybe if I talk to her, she'll let me take the test again or do an extra report after I have studied the material."

1   **What will Emily probably do next?**

    A   She will talk to Mrs. Lambert.

    B   She will forget about the test.

    C   She will decide not to study history anymore.

    D   She will pretend she is sick.

Selection 2

Mr. Dimitriou looked at his car. It was covered with dust so deep he could write his name in it. He couldn't see out the front window. The side windows were dirty where his dog's nose had smushed against the glass. The back seat had piles of paper and an old umbrella on it. What a mess!

Mr. Dimitriou knew that he'd better do something about the car because he had plans with three friends tonight, and he was the driver. He and his friends were going to a basketball game.

2   **What do you think Mr. Dimitriou will probably do?**

    A   He will sell his car and buy a new one.

    B   He will cancel his plans with his friends.

    C   He will take the papers and umbrella out of the car.

    D   He will clean the back seat and take the car to a car wash.

NOTICE: Photocopying any part of this book is forbidden by law.

Selection 3

The last time there was a thunder and lightning storm, a huge bolt of lightning hit a tree down the block from Luis's house. Luis hadn't unplugged his modem or computer, and the sudden surge burned out his modem and damaged his computer. Now Luis listened nervously as thunder rumbled again.

"I need to do this research on the Internet," he thought. "But I can't take a chance on ruining my computer or modem again."

3 **What do you think Luis will do next?**

A   He will keep working on his computer.

B   He will unplug his computer and modem.

C   He will buy a new computer after the storm.

D   He will work in another room.

Selection 4

Yoshi had been waiting by the phone all day. Mr. Greenfeld had promised he'd call today, one way or the other. Yoshi hoped it would be good news. He really wanted this job. He knew he was one of three applicants, but he felt he had a good chance. He'd done a good job on the skills test, he had experience in this kind of work, and he thought the interview had gone very well. The money they were offering was not as much as Yoshi had made in his old job, but he knew he'd have good opportunities here. If he just could get the job, he knew he would do well.

The phone rang! It was Mr. Greenfeld. "Well, Yoshi," he said. "If you would like to work for our company, the job is yours."

4 **What do you think Yoshi will say?**

A   "No thank you. It is not enough money."

B   "Yes, I will accept the job."

C   "No, I already have a job."

D   "I have to think about this."

NOTICE: Photocopying any part of this book is forbidden by law.

12 JUDGING AUTHOR'S PURPOSE AND POINT OF VIEW

GETTING THE IDEA

Authors have a purpose, or reason, in mind when they write.

- Authors may want to **inform**. A how-to book informs by giving instructions to readers on how to make or do something.

- Authors may want to **entertain**. A joke book entertains, or amuses, by making readers laugh.

- Authors may want to **persuade**. To *persuade* means to convince someone to think or act in a certain way. An advertisement tries to convince readers to buy a product or use a certain service.

Sometimes an author may have more than one purpose. For instance, an author may wish to inform, but do so in a way that also entertains. However, there is usually one main purpose which predominates.

The way an author feels about a topic is called the author's **point of view**. Sometimes the point of view is clearly stated, but most often you will need to decide it for yourself.

Some questions on the test will ask you about an author's purpose and point of view. The questions might look like the ones shown below.

- What is the purpose of this passage?

- The author's purpose for this passage is _____.

- Which statement below best describes the author's view of _____?

- The author seems to feel that _____.

The examples that follow will help you learn how to answer these kinds of questions.

NOTICE: Photocopying any part of this book is forbidden by law.

AUTHOR'S PURPOSE

You can usually decide the purpose by first thinking about the way a selection is written. You can ask yourself these kinds of questions:

- Does this selection present facts?

- Does this selection give steps and pictures for how to make or do something?

- Does this selection inform about a news event or announce another kind of event?

- Does this selection tell an exciting, scary, or funny story?

- Does this selection try to convince me about something? What is the author trying to make me think, or feel, or do?

Decide the author's purpose for each example that follows.

Example 1

Here is a zesty recipe to make baked beans. Cook 1 cup of chopped onion with 1/4 pound of bacon until the bacon is browned. Stir in two 16-ounce cans of baked beans in tomato sauce. Add 1/3 cup of yellow mustard and 1/4 cup of brown sugar. Heat to a boil. Reduce heat and simmer 15 minutes.

 The author wrote this passage to

A   instruct people on the health benefits of beans

B   give directions for cooking baked beans

C   discuss various ways to cook beans

D   amuse people with a story about beans

The correct answer is Choice **B**. Directions for cooking usually give specific information on what ingredients to add and how long to cook something. This selection gives specific directions for a baked beans recipe.

NOTICE: Photocopying any part of this book is forbidden by law.

Example 2

"You folks just don't know what a hot summer is," said Abe. "Why, when I was young, we had summers so hot, we had to hose down the corn plants to keep 'em from turning into popcorn. And it was so hot you could fry an egg on the sidewalk."

"That's nothing, Abe," countered Zeke. "Why, when I was a boy, summers were so hot the eggs the hens laid were already hard boiled."

2 **What is the author's purpose in writing this selection?**

   A   to give readers facts about summer temperatures

   B   to advise readers how to make popcorn

   C   to convince readers that summers were hotter in the past

   D   to entertain readers with silly stories

Choice **D** is the correct answer. The exaggeration in the story is a clue that it is a "tall tale," a story that uses exaggeration to entertain.

Example 3

Many pets live with stress. The pet's failure to cope with this stress is at the root of many behavior problems. One way to help your pet cope is through massage—petting a cat or dog with firm, long strokes while talking in a soothing voice. Try it on your pet. The soothing effects of massage usually help to establish a bond of trust between animal and owner.

3 **What is the author's purpose in writing this selection?**

   A   to convince the reader of the joys of owning a pet

   B   to explain why dogs may have behavior problems

   C   to convince readers that massage can benefit a pet

   D   to establish a bond of trust between the writer and the pet

Choice **C** is the correct answer. The writer tries to convince the reader by giving reasons why massaging a pet is good for both owner and pet.

NOTICE: Photocopying any part of this book is forbidden by law.

AUTHOR'S POINT OF VIEW

You can figure out what an author thinks of or feels about a person, animal, event, or idea by noticing the kinds of words he or she uses. For example,

- Suppose an author uses words such as *skillful*, *strong*, and *graceful* when describing a person. These words are clues that the author admires the person.

- Suppose an author uses words such as *annoying*, *frustrating*, and *irritating*. These words are clues that the author doesn't like, or is critical of the person.

The kinds of examples an author uses to describe a person, animal, event, or idea will also give you clues about an author's feelings. You will know whether the examples show positive or negative attitudes.

Decide the author's point of view for the examples that follow.

Example 4

If you want a pet that is beautiful, affectionate, and intelligent, get a cat. Cats do not require a great deal of space, nor do they have to be walked daily. For this reason cats are excellent pets for small apartments. A cat can be left alone for a weekend, too. Just be sure it has food, water, and a clean litter box. Your cat will get along fine without you, though it will most likely greet you warmly when you return.

4 **The author seems to feel that**

A cats make terrific pets

B people should go away for the weekend

C cats are not affectionate

D people should not keep cats in apartments

The author gives many reasons in support of cats as pets. In addition, the author uses many positive words such as *beautiful* and *affectionate* to describe cats. Choice **A** is the correct answer.

NOTICE: Photocopying any part of this book is forbidden by law.

Example 5

Fifty years ago, before televisions were a common feature of every home, families would gather in the living room after supper. They would play a game or sing songs around the piano. Sometimes they would gather around the radio to listen to a comedy or mystery show. These activities required imagination and creativity, and they brought families together. Much of television, on the other hand, makes people into passive, solitary viewers and requires little imagination. In addition, since many children have their own televisions in their rooms, parents often have no idea what programs their children are watching.

5 **How does the author feel about television?**

A Watching television requires imagination and creativity.

B Most television programs are not inspiring in any way.

C Television has comedy and mystery shows.

D There are absolutely no worthwhile programs on television.

The writer uses negative words to describe television: *solitary, passive*. In addition, the writer contrasts the activities of families before television as requiring imagination and says that they brought families together. The statements about television indicate that the correct answer is Choice **B**.

Example 6

Go see *Write Back Soon*. This movie is more than a romantic comedy or a tender love story. It is a thought-provoking movie, a touching look into the development of a long-distance friendship between two people from completely different backgrounds. It features excellent camera work and superb performances from Janna Allison and Bradley Whitfield. We are sure to hear more from these wonderful new talents.

6 **Which sentence best explains the writer's view of the movie *Write Back Soon*?**

A It is thought-provoking, but the acting is not good.

B It is extremely funny.

C It is thought-provoking and touching, with wonderful performances.

D It is completely different, but not worth seeing.

The correct answer is Choice **C**. The writer uses many positive words in this passage: *thought-provoking, touching,* and *excellent camera work*.

 NOTICE: Photocopying any part of this book is forbidden by law.

Sometimes the test will have questions about a passage that ask for both the author's purpose and point of view. The following example shows this.

Example 7

To the Editor:

The Town Planning Board of Millville wants us to believe that the new Wall King Shopping Center would be a wonderful thing for our town. But this shopping center will bring additional traffic to our already congested roads. In addition, the site for this center sits a mere 100 yards from a stream which feeds into Lake Wacopee, a beautiful natural lake teeming with fish. Should we take a chance on polluting this lake?

Besides the threat to the environment, consider the impact of this superstore on local businesses. We already have a local pharmacy and two small markets. Do we really want this new shopping center to drive our local stores out of business?

Let the Planning Board know how you feel. Write and voice your opposition!

7A **What is the purpose of this passage?**

A to gather support for the new shopping center

B to persuade readers to oppose the new shopping center

C to entertain people with a funny story about a shopping center

D to inform readers about fishing in Lake Wacopee

The correct answer is Choice **B**. The author gives reasons to oppose the shopping center and asks people to write to the Planning Board to voice their opposition.

7B **What is the author's point of view?**

A The writer is in favor of the new shopping center.

B The writer is a member of the Millville Planning Board.

C The writer thinks we pay too much attention to the environment.

D The writer sees the new shopping center as a bad idea.

The correct answer is Choice **D**. The writer gives reasons the shopping center would be bad for both the environment and for local businesses.

 Your teacher will discuss your answer.

NOTICE: Photocopying any part of this book is forbidden by law.

TIPS AND STRATEGIES FOR JUDGING AUTHOR'S PURPOSE AND POINT OF VIEW

☛ The reason why an author writes a selection is called the **author's purpose**.

☛ Authors write for three main purposes: to **inform**, to **entertain**, or to **persuade**. Ask yourself questions about the kind of writing being used. Based on your answers to these questions, you can decide the purpose.

- If you read a selection that has facts about a topic (names, dates, places, events), you know it is written mostly to inform.

- If you read a story selection that has characters, events, and dialogue, you know it is mostly meant to entertain.

- If you read an advertisement or a newspaper editorial, you know that it is written mostly to persuade.

☛ The way an author seems to feel about a topic is called the author's **point of view**. Sometimes an author will reveal his or her feelings directly. Usually you must figure it out.

☛ Pay attention to the kinds of words an author uses. Words such as *best*, *foolish*, *delicate*, *funny*, *boring*, *aggravating*, and *fascinating* will give you clues about the author's feelings.

☛ Pay attention to the kinds of examples an author gives to explain or describe a person, animal, event, or idea. Notice whether the examples are positive or negative. These clues will also help you know what an author feels. An author may include both good and bad points, but usually one will predominate. See which "side" the author seems to be on.

☛ Knowing the author's purpose and point of view will help you better understand and appreciate what you are reading.

NOTICE: Photocopying any part of this book is forbidden by law.

SELECTIONS FOR PRACTICE

Selection 1

When we first moved to the house on Brookfield Lane, everything seemed normal. However, after a few months, odd things began to happen. First, I noticed that the window in the back bedroom would not stay closed. I would close it carefully before going to bed, but in the morning it was always open about six inches from the bottom. Then I noticed the stain in the bathroom sink. No matter how I scrubbed it, it always returned.

Then there were the noises. With five of us living in the house, I seldom had it to myself. But one afternoon everyone was out except me. I was working in my downstairs office, concentrating hard, and only half-heard the footsteps in the upstairs hall. But gradually I became aware of someone walking from the back bedroom to the stairs, then back the other way. I thought, "Oh, it's one of the kids." Then I realized with a shock—there wasn't anyone home, except me.

1 **What is the author's purpose for writing this passage?**

A to explain why a window remained open

B to entertain people with a strange story

C to persuade people not to visit her

D to explain how to clean a sink

Selection 2

The Patterson Library needs help. Did you know that most towns in our state spend about thirty dollars per year for each resident for the town library? But our town gives our library only eleven dollars a year. This is ridiculous! It is not enough to supply the library with the funds it needs to provide the service our residents deserve. The budget increase is a positive step towards improving our library. Give it your support!

2 **The author seems to feel that**

A the library is not being given enough money and needs more

B the library budget increase is ridiculous

C the library has more than enough money now

D the residents do not deserve a better library

NOTICE: Photocopying any part of this book is forbidden by law.

Selection 3

The idea of public school uniforms is an idea whose time has come. There are some people who object to school uniforms because they say they will stifle a student's creativity and self-expression. This is silly nonsense. There are plenty of other ways for students to express themselves. Besides, many artists and writers have come from schools where uniforms were required. Uniforms certainly didn't inhibit their creativity.

School uniforms have many things going for them. First, they eliminate the differences between kids who can afford the latest in designer fashions and those who can't. No one will be "ranked" by what they can afford to wear. Second, wearing a uniform will do away with kids dressing in gang colors. Third, wearing a uniform will make kids feel like they belong to their school and instill a feeling of school pride. Fourth, uniforms are neater than the sloppy clothes some kids wear. Kids will get used to dressing the way they will need to dress for the workplace.

3A **Why do you think the author wrote this passage?**

A as an advertisement for a store that sells school uniforms

B to persuade readers not to wear designer clothes

C to persuade people not to support the idea of school uniforms

D to persuade people that school uniforms are a good idea

3B **Which statement best expresses the author's point of view on the subject of school uniforms?**

A School uniforms stifle students' creativity and freedom of expression.

B School uniforms are nicer than designer fashions.

C School uniforms eliminate differences based on what students can afford, and they instill school pride.

D School uniforms are a good means of self-expression.

NOTICE: Photocopying any part of this book is forbidden by law.

PART 5: WRITING STRATEGIES

NOTICE: Photocopying any part of this book is forbidden by law.

109

13 IDENTIFYING TOPIC, SUPPORTING, AND CONCLUDING SENTENCES

You know that a paragraph is a group of sentences about a topic. A paragraph that is clear and well written has a topic sentence, supporting sentences, and a concluding sentence.

- A **topic sentence** begins the paragraph. It names the topic and tells the most important idea about it. The topic sentence lets readers know what the paragraph is about.

- The sentences that follow the topic sentence are called **supporting sentences**. Each of these sentences explains more about the idea expressed in the topic sentence.

- A **concluding sentence** is the last sentence in the paragraph. This sentence sums up the ideas in the paragraph.

The paragraph below is labeled to show you the parts. Read the paragraph.

Topic Sentence ➡   Stephen King is a well-known writer of horror novels. He has written more than forty books and

Supporting Sentences ➡   many short stories. Critics have praised his work, and his books have sold very well. Many of his novels and stories have been made into films or

Concluding Sentence ➡   television features. He is certainly one of today's most successful writers.

On the test you will be asked to choose a topic, supporting, or concluding sentence that best fits in a paragraph. Once you choose an answer, be sure to reread the paragraph with your choice to be sure it makes sense. Try the examples on the next page.

In this first example, the blank is at the beginning of the paragraph. This lets you know that the question will be about a topic sentence.

 NOTICE: Photocopying any part of this book is forbidden by law.

Example 1

_____. The first flutes were simple tubes of bamboo. They had finger holes and were held vertically. Later, the transverse, or horizontal, flute was developed in Germany. Then about 1670, flute makers began to make changes to it. They made the flute out of boxwood in three sections and added keys. Now the flute could play all the sharps and flats in the scale.

1 **Choose the topic sentence that best fits in the paragraph.**

A The flute is a very popular instrument.

B Today's flute has changed greatly from long ago.

C The flute can play in any musical key.

D My favorite instrument is the flute.

The best topic sentence is Choice **B**. It states that the flute has changed from long ago. The rest of the paragraph tells how the flute has changed.

In the next example, you are asked to choose a supporting sentence that best fits in the paragraph. To help you decide, think about the idea expressed in the topic sentence. Also see what the facts in the other supporting sentences explain about the topic sentence.

Example 2

Did you know electronic music was invented a hundred years ago? _____. It was called the Dynamaphone. It used dynamos, machines that convert mechanical energy into electrical energy, to produce sounds. The sounds were then sent over telephone lines to restaurants, hotels, and private homes.

2 **Choose the sentence that best fills the blank.**

A Today many bands use electronic keyboards.

B Electric guitars became popular in the 1950s.

C Thaddeus Cahill created the first important electronic instrument in 1906.

D The Dynamaphone weighed 200 tons.

NOTICE: Photocopying any part of this book is forbidden by law.

The supporting sentence that best fits is Choice **C**. This sentence tells who invented the first electronic instrument and when it was invented. The other supporting sentences tell about the instrument.

The next two examples ask you to choose the best concluding sentence. You can tell because the blank is at the end of each paragraph. This last sentence of a paragraph ties together all the facts.

Example 3

Packing for a trip is never easy, but here are some tips that will help you pack more effectively. Bring clothes that are lightweight and blend in color so that you can mix and match. Put heavy things, such as shoes, on the bottom of your suitcase. Roll up knits so they don't wrinkle. Most important, don't bring too much. _____.

3 **Which sentence best fills the blank in the paragraph?**

A Put shoes in plastic bags.

B Some people take several trips a year.

C Bring things that can be washed and dried easily.

D Follow these tips for hassle-free packing.

The best concluding sentence is Choice **D**. It relates back to the topic sentence that mentions packing tips and sums up the ideas about packing.

Example 4

Perhaps you have wondered where our image of "Uncle Sam," a symbol of our country, came from. Back in 1812, merchant Samuel Wilson stamped "U.S." on barrels being shipped to the army. His friends teased him that the letters stood for his nickname, "Uncle Sam," rather than for "United States." Then during World War I, artist James Flagg used himself as a model for a recruiting poster that showed "Uncle Sam" saying "I want you for the U.S. Army." _____.

NOTICE: Photocopying any part of this book is forbidden by law.

4   **Which sentence best fills the blank in the paragraph?**

A   The bearded man in a top hat became our "Uncle Sam."

B   Other countries have symbols, too.

C   Another symbol of the United States is the bald eagle.

D   Uncle Sam is a good nickname.

The best concluding sentence is Choice **A**. It relates back to the topic sentence that mentions "Uncle Sam," and sums up the ideas about him.

TIPS AND STRATEGIES FOR IDENTIFYING TOPIC, SUPPORTING, AND CONCLUDING SENTENCES

☞ Remember that a clear and well-written paragraph has a topic sentence, supporting sentences, and a concluding sentence.

- A **topic sentence** is the first sentence in the paragraph. It names the topic of the paragraph and tells the most important idea about it.

- The sentences that follow the topic sentence are called **supporting sentences**. They give more details about the idea expressed in the topic sentence.

- A **concluding sentence** is the last sentence in the paragraph. This sentence sums up the ideas in the paragraph. The concluding sentence might add a fact that ties all the facts together.

☞ On the test, look for where the blank is placed in the paragraph. This will help you know whether you are to choose a topic sentence, supporting sentence, or concluding sentence. Sometimes there may be no blank, and you will be asked to choose which sentence best follows a particular sentence. Based on the location of the sentence, you should still be able to figure out whether you are to choose a topic, supporting, or concluding sentence.

☞ Once you choose an answer, reread the paragraph with your choice to be sure it makes sense.

SELECTIONS FOR PRACTICE

Selection 1

_____. This pesticide was used in the mid-1900s to kill insects that harmed crops. But DDT seeped into rivers and streams and eventually reached the ocean. Fish in the ocean absorbed the DDT, and it stayed in their bodies. Bald eagles ate the polluted fish, and the DDT stayed in their bodies, too. The eagles began to lay eggs that had soft shells. When the mother eagles sat on the eggs, they broke. Those young eaglets which did hatch were often unable to produce their own young.

1   **Choose the topic sentence that best fits in the paragraph.**

    A   The bald eagle is our national bird.

    B   A pesticide called DDT almost wiped out the bald eagle.

    C   These soft shells made the eaglets vulnerable.

    D   There are many pesticides still on the market.

Selection 2

Hatshepsut was one of the few female rulers of ancient Egypt. She was a princess and the wife of a pharaoh, or king. When her husband died, her ten-year-old stepson was supposed to become pharaoh. _____. So she was named co-ruler. She ruled for about 15 years, until her death in 1458 BC.

2   **Choose the sentence that best fits the blank in the paragraph.**

    A   Hatshepsut means "Foremost of the Noble Ladies."

    B   Hatshepsut organized a trading expedition to the south.

    C   Hatshepsut said he was too young to rule on his own.

    D   There were only a few women rulers in Egypt.

 NOTICE: Photocopying any part of this book is forbidden by law.

Selection 3

A favorite flower of the Sultan Süleyman was the tulip, named for the Turkish word for *turban*. In the 1560s, an ambassador to Süleyman's court gave some tulip bulbs to a Dutch gardener. The rare flowers became very much in demand. The Dutch farmers started to grow them to sell.

3 **Which sentence best follows the last sentence in the paragraph?**

A Today the Dutch are the world's leading growers of tulips.

B Tulips come in many beautiful colors.

C Turkish was the language spoken in Süleyman's country.

D Süleyman was ruler of the Ottoman Empire.

Selection 4

_____. Her novels featuring her two famous detectives, Hercule Poirot and Miss Jane Marple, have been translated into more than one hundred languages. Many of Christie's books were made into movies or filmed for television. She also wrote several plays, including *The Mousetrap*, which is still running in London after fifty years! By the time she died in 1976, Agatha Christie was the best-selling English novelist of all time.

4 **Which sentence makes the best topic sentence for the paragraph?**

A Agatha Christie was a well-known British mystery writer.

B Many people enjoy reading mystery novels.

C Agatha Christie's books can be found in libraries.

D I have read several books by Agatha Christie.

NOTICE: Photocopying any part of this book is forbidden by law.

14 ORDERING IDEAS IN SENTENCES

Ideas in a paragraph need to be connected and hold together to make sense. So the **sequence**, or **order**, of ideas is very important. That order begins with a topic sentence that introduces the main idea about the topic. Then there are the supporting sentences. Finally, there is a concluding sentence that ties all the ideas together.

To help you on the test, the last lesson taught you about choosing the best topic, supporting, or concluding sentence. But there are also some test items that ask you to tell *where* a sentence will best fit in a paragraph.

Here is what a test question will look like. You see that the sentences are numbered.

▼1 With an altitude of 29, 028 feet, Mount Everest is the tallest mountain in the world. ▼2 Everest is actually a giant among giants. ▼3 It is in the Himalayas, Earth's highest and youngest mountains. ▼4 In fact, the fourteen highest peaks in the world are found there.

Where would this new sentence best fit in the paragraph?

So Mount Everest is truly at the top of the world.

A after Sentence 1

B after Sentence 2

C after Sentence 3

D after Sentence 4

NOTICE: Photocopying any part of this book is forbidden by law.

The first sentence of the example paragraph introduces the topic of Mount Everest as the tallest mountain in the world. The next few sentences explain that Everest is the tallest of a range of very tall mountains. The new sentence begins with the word *so*, which is a clue to expect a conclusion. It then sums up the paragraph, saying Everest is truly at the top of the world. The sentence belongs at the end of the paragraph. The correct answer is Choice **D**.

You can reread the paragraph and include the new sentence to check that the order of ideas makes sense.

Try this example. After you read the paragraph and new sentence, think about the order of ideas presented.

Example 1

▼¹ Fifth- and sixth-graders at Westford Central School in Westford, Vermont, did real archaeology on an archaeological site near their school. ▼² Archaeology is the study of the remains of past cultures. ▼³ Maybe the word makes you think of someone uncovering a lost tomb in Egypt. ▼⁴ Or you may think of someone studying a Roman ruin in Italy. ▼⁵ The Vermont students learned that history is under their own feet, too.

4 **Where would this sentence best fit in the paragraph?**

But history doesn't only happen in far-off places.

A   after Sentence 2

B   after Sentence 3

C   after Sentence 4

D   after Sentence 5

NOTICE: Photocopying any part of this book is forbidden by law.

Sentences 3 and 4 remind you that archaeology is often about far-off places such as Egypt or Italy. However, the word *But* in the new sentence is a clue that this sentence presents a contrasting idea. A logical place for it is *after* the ideas it contrasts with. The correct answer is Choice **C**, after Sentence 4.

Reread the paragraph and include the new sentence to check that the order of ideas makes sense.

Now try Examples 2 and 3.

Example 2

▼1 To begin with, giraffes are the tallest of all animals.
▼2 Males may grow more than eighteen feet tall. ▼3 The giraffe gets most of its height from its six-foot legs. ▼4 Its neck may be even longer. ▼5 In addition, the giraffe has a long twenty-one-inch tongue it uses to strip leaves from trees.

2 **Where would this sentence best fit in the paragraph?**

When you think of a giraffe, the words "tall" and "long" come to mind.

A before Sentence 1

B before Sentence 2

C before Sentence 3

D after Sentence 4

If you put the new sentence at the beginning, you see that it is a topic sentence. It states the topic of a giraffe being both tall and long. The rest of the paragraph gives several examples of ways the giraffe is both tall and long. Answer Choice **A** is correct.

NOTICE: Photocopying any part of this book is forbidden by law.

Example 3

▼1 In 1867, Secretary of State William H. Seward was ridiculed for buying Alaska from Russia. ▼2 People called Alaska "Seward's Folly," or "Seward's Polar Bear Garden." ▼3 Most people thought the price of $7, 200, 000 was outrageous. ▼4 They thought Alaska was a useless, frozen land. ▼5 It wasn't until many years later that people realized what a bargain Seward really obtained.

3 **Where would this sentence best fit in the paragraph?**

They wondered why anyone in his right mind would want to go there.

A before Sentence 1

B after Sentence 1

C after Sentence 4

D after Sentence 5

Sentence 1 introduces the idea of Seward being ridiculed for buying Alaska. The new sentence supports this idea. The best place for it is after Sentence 4 because it follows the idea that Alaska was a useless, frozen land. Choice **C** is the correct answer.

TIPS AND STRATEGIES
FOR ORDERING IDEAS IN SENTENCES

☞ Remember that ideas in a paragraph need to be connected and hold together to make sense. So the **sequence**, or **order**, of ideas is very important.

☞ After you read a paragraph, think about the order of ideas presented. After reading the new sentence, decide whether it is a topic, supporting, or concluding sentence. Then see where it belongs in the paragraph.

☞ Remember to read the paragraph and include the new sentence to check that the order of all ideas makes sense.

NOTICE: Photocopying any part of this book is forbidden by law.

SELECTIONS FOR PRACTICE

Selection 1

▼¹ After the hardships of World War I (1914–1919), Americans wanted to enjoy themselves. ▼² In the 1920s, times were good, and many people had larger incomes. ▼³ People had more free time, too, as workers won the fight for a shorter work day. ▼⁴ A new kind of music called "jazz" swept the nation. ▼⁵ One writer described the time as the liveliest party in history.

1 **Where would this sentence best fit in the paragraph?**

The decade became known as "The Roaring Twenties."

A after Sentence 1
B after Sentence 3
C after Sentence 4
D after Sentence 5

Selection 2

▼¹ Icebergs are white because the ice from which they are made is full of tiny air bubbles. ▼² These bubbled surfaces reflect white light. ▼³ They cause the iceberg to have an overall white appearance. ▼⁴ Melted water sometimes refreezes as clear ice in the crevices of an iceberg. ▼⁵ This bubble-free ice scatters the light and appears blue, just as the sky appears blue.

 NOTICE: Photocopying any part of this book is forbidden by law.

2 | **Where would this sentence best fit in the paragraph?**

Most icebergs appear to be white, or sometimes streaked with blue.

A   before Sentence 1

B   before Sentence 2

C   after Sentence 3

D   after Sentence 4

Selection 3

▼[1]One major hazard in climbing at high altitudes is the lack of oxygen. ▼[2]Humans must have oxygen to live. ▼[3]Oxygen makes up only about twenty-one percent of the air we breathe. ▼[4]But the higher up a mountain a climber goes, the less atmospheric pressure there is. ▼[5]That means there is less oxygen available to breathe. ▼[6]At 18,000 feet, the amount of oxygen is half that at sea level. ▼[7]Climbers soon begin to feel the effects of too little oxygen. ▼[8]The lack of oxygen causes headaches, mental confusion, and impaired judgment.

3 | **Where would this sentence best fit in the paragraph?**

At the summit of Everest (29, 028 feet) the air contains less than one-third of the oxygen at sea level.

A   after Sentence 2

B   after Sentence 4

C   after Sentence 6

D   after Sentence 8

NOTICE: Photocopying any part of this book is forbidden by law.

15 IDENTIFYING RELEVANT INFORMATION

GETTING THE IDEA

In the last lesson, you worked on ordering the ideas in a paragraph. This is an important writing strategy. It is just as important to make sure that the information in a paragraph is about the same topic. All the ideas in a paragraph should **relate to** and support the topic sentence.

Some test questions will ask you to find the sentence that does not belong in a given paragraph. A sentence about a cat in a paragraph about what to feed a pet rabbit would clearly not belong. But the paragraphs on the test are not that easy!

Here is what a test item might look like.

1 Alexander Calder was a sculptor most famous for his moving sculptures, called "mobiles." 2 The mobiles are made of painted sheet-aluminum, brass, and steel wired together. 3 They are delicately balanced so that they move in the breeze and create ever-changing patterns. 4 Calder was born in Philadelphia, Pennsylvania and studied art in New York City. 5 Calder's mobiles decorate parks and public settings in cities such as Brussels, New York, Montreal, and Chicago.

Which sentence does not belong?

A	**B**	**C**	**D**
Sentence 2	Sentence 3	Sentence 4	Sentence 5

NOTICE: Photocopying any part of this book is forbidden by law.

You can see that the topic sentence in the paragraph is about Alexander Calder's mobiles. Sentences 2, 3, and 5 give more **relevant**, or **related**, information about Calder's mobiles.

Sentence 4, however, tells about where Calder was born and studied. This is factual, and about Calder, but it does not belong in this paragraph. It does not connect with the topic sentence or the other sentences in the paragraph. The correct answer is Choice **C**.

Now try the next two examples.

Example 1

¹From the Civil War until the late 1890s, Thomas Nast was the most powerful political cartoonist in America. ²He is best known for his cartoon campaign against "Boss Tweed," a dishonest New York City politician who cost the city millions of dollars. ³Other big cities had problems with corrupt officials, too. ⁴Nast drew many cartoons which showed what Tweed and his supporters were up to. ⁵The drawings had a powerful effect on public opinion, and eventually Tweed landed in jail.

1 **Which sentence does not belong?**

A	**B**	**C**	**D**
Sentence 2	Sentence 3	Sentence 4	Sentence 5

Choice **B** is the correct answer. All the sentences except Sentence 3 tell information about Nast's political cartoons. A sentence about corruption in other cities is off the topic.

NOTICE: Photocopying any part of this book is forbidden by law.

Example 2

▼1 Although your cat cannot speak your language, your cat's tail will give you clues to what your cat is trying to communicate. ▼2 A tail held straight up means all is well. ▼3 But if the tip of the tail is beginning to twitch, watch out—the cat is getting annoyed. ▼4 If the tail is thumping hard and wildly, the cat is angry. ▼5 A cat's meow can express different things, too.

2 **Which sentence does not belong?**

A Sentence 2   **B** Sentence 3   **C** Sentence 4   **D** Sentence 5

Choice **D** is the correct answer. All sentences except sentence 5 tell about how a cat uses its tail to express what it is feeling. Sentence 5 could be the topic sentence of another paragraph.

TIPS AND STRATEGIES
FOR IDENTIFYING RELEVANT INFORMATION

☞ Remember that all the sentences in a paragraph should be about the same topic. All the information should be **relevant** to the topic sentence.

☞ Think about the idea in the topic sentence. See what information that explains the topic stated is given in the other sentences. Decide which sentence does not contain information about this main idea.

NOTICE: Photocopying any part of this book is forbidden by law.

SELECTIONS FOR PRACTICE

Selection 1

▼[1] A classic American toy that has been around for more than fifty years was actually invented by accident. ▼[2] James Wright was an engineer working to develop an artificial rubber, and he mixed silicone oil and boric acid. ▼[3] Many other things have been invented by accident, too. ▼[4] The result was a silly, putty-like substance that bounced! ▼[5] No practical use was ever found for it, but a toy manufacturer saw its possibilities and began to sell it in plastic eggs at a toy fair.

1 **Which sentence does not belong?**

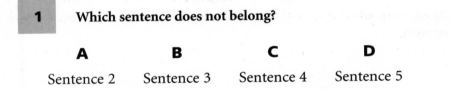

A	B	C	D
Sentence 2	Sentence 3	Sentence 4	Sentence 5

NOTICE: Photocopying any part of this book is forbidden by law.

Selection 2

▼Children in Ancient Rome did not attend public schools, but were taught at home by a parent or a servant until they were six. ▼Many children today are home-schooled. ▼Roman boys and some girls were sent to private schools where they learned reading, writing, and arithmetic. ▼Wealthy children might continue their education until age fourteen, with the emphasis on Latin and Greek grammar, literature, mathematics, music, and astronomy. ▼Higher education meant studying rhetoric—the art of public speaking— and this was only for upper-class boys who planned a career in law or politics.

2 **Which sentence does not belong?**

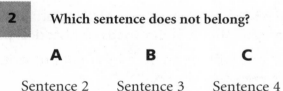

A **B** **C** **D**

Sentence 2   Sentence 3   Sentence 4   Sentence 5

 NOTICE: Photocopying any part of this book is forbidden by law.

16 IDENTIFYING SOURCES OF INFORMATION

You know that information can be found in a variety of sources. There are nonfiction books about every topic. There are textbooks that cover many subjects, such as social studies, science, and math. There are how-to books, newspapers, and reference books such as dictionaries, encyclopedias, atlases, and almanacs.

These sources are mostly found in printed form. But information may also be found on the **Internet** or viewed as **videos** or on **film**.

What kind of source will best help you find the information you need? Knowing the answer to this question is an important strategy for reading as well as writing. For example, you know that

- a **dictionary** and **thesaurus** give information about words
- an **encyclopedia** gives information about a whole range of topics
- an **atlas** contains maps of the whole world or of a region and also gives facts; special atlases might be about roads or historical places
- an **almanac** is a yearly book with up-to-date information, including important dates and the weather

On the test you will find questions that ask you to identify a good source of information about a given topic. A test item might look like the one below.

The ancient Romans loved to watch contests of physical skill. Our word *circus* comes from the Latin word for a large circular ring or arena where races and other events took place. Chariot races, gladiator fights, and contests with wild animals were all popular.

In which source would you look to find out more about entertainment in ancient Rome?

A   dictionary

B   thesaurus

C   atlas

D   encyclopedia

NOTICE: Photocopying any part of this book is forbidden by law.

Choice **D** is the correct answer. Encyclopedias contain articles with information about a great many topics.

A test item might ask two questions about a passage that involve choosing the best sources of information.

Example 1

Ancient Egypt grew up along the Nile, the world's longest river. The Nile begins in the snow-capped mountains of East Africa. It flows north for 4,000 miles until it reaches the Mediterranean Sea. There the river divides into several branches, forming a fan-shaped delta.

1A In which source would you look to find out the country in which the Nile River begins?

    A   a dictionary

    B   an atlas

    C   a newspaper

    D   a thesaurus

Choice **B** is correct. An atlas is a book of maps. You would look at a map of Africa to find where the Nile River originates.

1B Which of the following books would be most likely to give more information about Ancient Egypt?

    A   *Exploring Central Africa*

    B   *Land of the Pharaohs*

    C   *The World's Rivers*

    D   *Egypt in the Twentieth Century*

Choice **B** is correct. You probably know that the pharaohs were kings of ancient Egypt. Of the four titles, this book is most likely to have information about Ancient Egypt.

 NOTICE: Photocopying any part of this book is forbidden by law.

Other test items might not give a paragraph first. Instead, a question might be part of several questions about a long selection. The next two examples show these kinds of questions.

Example 2

2A **If you wanted to know people's opinions about China's bid to hold the 2008 Olympic Games, which of these resources would be most helpful?**

    A   a dictionary

    B   a general encyclopedia

    C   a newspaper

    D   a world atlas

The correct answer is Choice **C**. A newspaper has day-to-day coverage of news events and editorials.

2B **If you wanted to find out who won the women's 400-meter race at the 2000 Summer Olympics, which would be the best resource?**

    A   a nonfiction book on the history of the Olympics

    B   an almanac published after 2000

    C   a chart showing how many medals each country won

    D   a general encyclopedia article on the Olympic Games

Choice **B** is the best answer. An almanac gives statistics on many subjects, including names of winners of athletic competitions.

NOTICE: Photocopying any part of this book is forbidden by law.

You know that you can often find information in more than one source. But some sources are more current and accurate than others. You need to decide the most current and accurate source to answer the following question.

Example 3

3 **Which of the following would give the most accurate and current information about recent important events in the Caribbean?**

A a book called *Tropical Paradises*, published in 1968

B this week's issue of a weekly news magazine

C a book called *Exploring the Caribbean*, published last year

D a novel set in the Caribbean

Choices A and C are not current. Choice D, a novel, would not be a reliable source. It is fiction. Of the sources listed, a weekly news magazine is most likely to be current and reliable. Choice **B** is the correct answer.

TIPS AND STRATEGIES
FOR IDENTIFYING SOURCES OF INFORMATION

☞ Remember that different sources of information serve different purposes. For example, a **dictionary** is the best source to find the meaning of a word. An **encyclopedia** is the best source to find facts about a topic. An **atlas** contains maps and facts about particular places. A **biography** will give in-depth information about a person. An **almanac** is a good source for statistics and recent information.

☞ Some sources can give you more complete information than other sources. Some sources give you more accurate and current information than other sources. For these reasons:

• Be sure you consider sources carefully when you do your own research reports. Check publication dates to see how current a source is.

• When answering a test question, think carefully about what the question is asking.

• Review the answer choices carefully, too. Think about the kind of information each source gives before choosing an answer.

 NOTICE: Photocopying any part of this book is forbidden by law.

SELECTIONS FOR PRACTICE

Selection 1

Mohandas Gandhi was an influential Indian leader who lived from 1869 to 1948. Because of his simple life and his religious principles, Gandhi was known by the Hindi word *Mahatma*, which means "great soul." During his life, he worked to free India from British rule. He used a form of nonviolent protest called "civil disobedience." His methods influenced many later leaders, including Rev. Martin Luther King, Jr.

1A   **Which source below would be the best place to find more information about the life of Gandhi?**

A   a magazine article about India

B   a social studies text book

C   a biography of Gandhi

D   the biography section of a dictionary

1B   **Which book would most likely have the most complete information about India's struggle for independence?**

A   *Famous Places in India*

B   *India: The Path to Freedom*

C   *Great World Leaders*

D   *Festivals of India*

NOTICE: Photocopying any part of this book is forbidden by law.

Selection 2

Have you ever seen a wombat? What about a Tasmanian devil? Would you like your picture taken with a koala bear? These and other Australian mammals are all at the Taronga Park Zoo in Sydney, Australia. The zoo is open from 9 to 5 every day of the year and is just a short ferry ride across Sydney Harbor.

2A   **Which source below would be the best one to find the location of Sydney, Australia?**

     A   a world atlas

     B   a newspaper article about the Sydney Olympics

     C   an atlas of North America

     D   a nonfiction book about famous zoos

2B   **Which source would probably have the most complete and current information about koalas?**

     A   *Bears I Have Known*, published in 1965

     B   "Mammals of Australia," a magazine article from 1976

     C   a novel called *The Enchanted Koala*

     D   *Life Cycle of the Koala*, published in 2002

NOTICE: Photocopying any part of this book is forbidden by law.

17 ORGANIZING INFORMATION

There are many reasons why you gather information from a source. You might just want to learn about a topic that interests you. You might need to write a report or make a booklet of some kind.

An important skill for organizing information is **outlining**. You know that an outline is a brief form of writing used to summarize topics, main ideas, and important details about a general topic. Roman numerals, letters, and numerals are used in an outline.

Since outlining is such a useful skill, the test has some questions that ask you to read and respond to an outline. A test item might look like Example 1 on the next page.

- Each Roman numeral names a topic.

- Each alphabet letter names what each main idea will be about when the report is written.

- Each numeral names an important detail under a main idea.

Be sure to read the outline at least twice to make sure you understand the information presented.

NOTICE: Photocopying any part of this book is forbidden by law.

Example 1

A group of students will attend Space Camp during spring break. Before they go, each student is writing a report on a space topic. Here is an outline a student prepared. Use the outline to answer the questions.

LIVING IN SPACE

I. _____

    A. Breathing

    B. Eating and Drinking

        1. types of food
        2. importance of liquids

    C. Sleeping

II. Working in Space

    A. Navigation and Control

    B. Conducting Scientific Research

    C. Assembling Space Stations

III. Communicating with the Earth

    A. Mission Control

    B. Computers in space

1A Which of these best fits next to Roman numeral I of the outline?

A Traveling in Space

B Meeting Basic Needs in Space

C First Humans in Space

D Getting to Space and Back

Choice **B** is the correct answer. Breathing, eating, drinking, and sleeping are all basic needs people have, so Choice **B** is the best topic.

NOTICE: Photocopying any part of this book is forbidden by law.

1B **Which section of the outline do these sentences best support?**

Astronauts carry out experiments in the low gravity of space. They are learning how gravity affects plants, animals, and humans.

A I-C

B II-B

C III-A

D III-B

Choice **B** is the correct answer. The two sentences tell about experiments the astronauts do. This fits under Topic II, Working in Space. Since experiments are a type of research, II-B is the best choice.

Example 2

Frances chose to write about volcanoes for a science report. She did some research and chose three main points to tell about. Here is the outline she made for her report. Use the outline to answer the questions on the next page.

VOLCANOES

I. How a Volcano is formed

    A. The Beginning of a Volcano

    B. _____

II. Kinds of Volcanoes

    A. Shield Volcanoes

    B. Cinder Cones

    C. Composite Volcanoes

III. Famous Volcanoes

    A. Mount Etna

        1. Located on the island of Sicily

        2. Europe's most active volcano

    B. Mount St. Helens

    C. Mount Pinatubo

NOTICE: Photocopying any part of this book is forbidden by law.

2A | **Which of these best fits next to Roman numeral I-B of the outline?**

    A   Mt. Ranier

    B   Active Volcanoes Today

    C   The Benefits of Volcanoes

    D   The Eruption of a Volcano

Choice **D** is the correct answer. The next logical idea after "the beginning of a volcano" is "the eruption of a volcano." None of the other three ideas fits the topic.

2B | **Which section of the outline does this sentence best support?**

The last serious eruptions of Mount Etna were in 1992 and 2001.

    A   I-A

    B   II-B

    C   III-A

    D   III-B

 Your teacher will discuss your answer.

 NOTICE: Photocopying any part of this book is forbidden by law.

TIPS AND STRATEGIES FOR ORGANIZING INFORMATION

☞ Remember that an **outline** is a brief form of writing—a list—used to summarize topics, main ideas, and important details about a general topic.

☞ Roman numerals, letters, and numerals are used in an outline. When you answer questions about an outline, or make an outline of your own, be sure that the details are organized under each main idea. You should also check that each main idea fits logically under its topic.

☞ Be sure to read the outline at least twice to make sure you understand the information presented.

NOTICE: Photocopying any part of this book is forbidden by law.

SELECTION FOR PRACTICE

Roberto was fascinated by wolves. He chose to do his research report about them. This is the outline he prepared. Use the outline to answer the questions.

THE WOLF

I. _____

    A. Timber Wolf

    B. Tundra Wolf

    C. Red Wolf

II. A Wolf's Life

    A. Habits of Wolves

    B. Raising Young

    C. Hunting

III. Wolves and People

    A. Fears and Problems

    B. Wolves in Literature

        1. Fairy Tales and Fables

        2. Sayings

NOTICE: Photocopying any part of this book is forbidden by law.

1A **Which of these headings best fits beside Roman numeral I of the outline?**

A   Where Wolves are Found

B   How Wolves are Related to Dogs

C   Kinds of Wolves

D   Fables about Wolves

1B **In which section of the outline would you place this information?**

In many fables and fairy tales, such as "Little Red Riding Hood," the wolf represents evil. The wolf is a symbol of evil in some old sayings, too. For instance, the expression "a wolf in sheep's clothing" means a person who acts friendly but who really intends harm.

A   II-A

B   II-B

C   III-A

D   III-B

PART 6: ANSWERING CONSTRUCTED-RESPONSE QUESTIONS

NOTICE: Photocopying any part of this book is forbidden by law.

18 WRITING SHORT ANSWERS

Besides multiple-choice questions, the TerraNova test has different kinds of **constructed-response,** or **open-ended, questions.** You use your own words to answer a question. Sometimes, you will be asked to write a few sentences. At other times, you will be asked to write something longer. This part of the *Coach* will help you learn and practice strategies for answering them.

GETTING THE IDEA

The test has three different kinds of **short-answer** questions:

1. A short-answer question will ask for details from a story or a selection that gives information. You will **write your answer in a few complete sentences** on blank lines given in the test booklet.

2. Another short-answer question might ask you to **fill in** some story details or facts on a **web** or **chart.**

3. A third kind of short-answer question asks you to **correct a paragraph** for **errors** in **spelling, punctuation, capitalization,** and **grammar.**

In this chapter, you will learn how to write each kind of short-answer question. Here are some good **tips for success:**

- Always read each question carefully to make sure you understand it.

- Underline key words in the question. You did this before, to answer multiple-choice questions. Underlining key words will help you answer open-ended questions, too. Underlining key words will help you stick to the topic.

- A question may have more than one part. Be sure you answer all parts.

NOTICE: Photocopying any part of this book is forbidden by law.

WRITING ANSWERS IN COMPLETE SENTENCES

You should write no more than three to five sentences for a short-answer question. Choose your words carefully so that each sentence helps to answer the question.

- In your first sentence, **use key words** from the question. Also **include at least one detail** that answers a part of the question.

- In the rest of your sentences, **add more details** that complete your answer to the question.

Example 1

Sea otters were once common along the north Pacific coast. California sea otters spend almost all their time in the water. Because the north Pacific is cold, they have developed beautiful, thick fur to keep warm. But fur traders began hunting sea otters for their thick fur. So many were hunted that by 1900 sea otters were nearly extinct. Today about 2,000 sea otters are left, and they are protected by law.

1   **Why did the sea otter almost become extinct? How are they now protected? Write a few sentences to explain. Use facts from the selection in your answer.**

Sea otters almost became extinct because hunters killed so many of them for their fur. The fur traders wanted them because sea otter fur is very thick and beautiful. The 2,000 or so sea otters left are protected by law.

This is a very good answer to the question. Do you know why?

- ✓ The writer told exactly why the sea otter almost became extinct. The first sentence uses the key words *sea otter*, *became*, and *extinct* from the question.

- ✓ The first sentence also tells the main reason or cause why the sea otter almost became extinct—because hunters killed them for their fur.

- ✓ The next two sentences explain why the fur was valuable and how they are now protected. All the details are from the selection.

NOTICE: Photocopying any part of this book is forbidden by law.

Here is an example with two different answers in complete sentences.

Example 2

Susan loved to ice skate. Her hero was Olympic champion Tara Lipinski, and Susan wanted to be like her. Susan knew that to even reach the Olympics she would have to work very hard.

Susan was certainly willing to work. Every morning she would get up at 4 AM to go to the ice skating rink. She would practice for two hours before going to school. After school she would have a lesson with her coach and then practice some more. Twice a week she took ballet lessons, too. Susan had little time for friends, but she didn't mind. She was determined to reach her goal.

2 **What was Susan's goal? What did she do to work toward this goal? Give details from the story to support your answer.**

Anna's answer

Susan wanted to skate like Tara Lipinski. I wouldn't want to get up at 4 A.M. to practice. I'm not good at skating anyway. I have weak ankles. I want to be a computer artist.

Sean's answer

Susan 's goal was to be an Olympic champion like her hero, Tara Lipinski. To work toward this goal, Susan got up at 4 A.M. to practice at the ice rink before school. She also had skating lessons and practice after school. Twice a week she took ballet lessons, too.

Which answer is better? Circle it. Now check (✓) the boxes below next to the reasons why it is better.

❑ It sticks to the topic asked about in the questions.

❑ It gives the important details from the selection.

❑ It does not give information that isn't asked for.

Sean's answer is better. All three boxes should be checked. Anna only answered part of the question. She did not include details from the story. Instead she told about herself.

 NOTICE: Photocopying any part of this book is forbidden by law.

FILLING IN ANSWERS ON A WEB OR CHART

Some short-answer questions will ask you to fill in a web or chart with details from the selection. Remember to **underline the key words** in the question. Also, **read the text** that is already **on the web or chart**. It will help you know what kinds of details belong in the empty places.

Example 3

After the Revolutionary War, our country was still not united. Our first government, the Articles of Confederation, gave almost all the power to the states. Each state could make its own laws, collect its own taxes, and makes its own money. But this quickly led to problems. Money printed in one state was not good in another state. People didn't think of themselves as being citizens of the United States, either. Instead they said, "I'm a New Yorker" or "I'm a Virginian." The Congress had no power to enforce the laws it passed. Even worse, it had no money—not even enough to pay the soldiers who had fought in the Revolution!

3 The selection says that the Articles of Confederation gave a lot of power to the states. What were the four main problems that this government caused? Fill in the boxes with details from the selection.

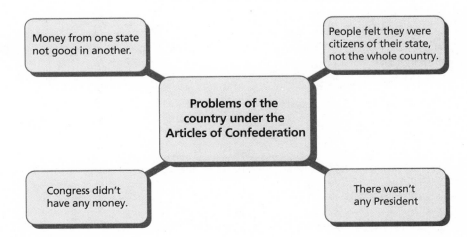

Money from one state not good in another.

People felt they were citizens of their state, not the whole country.

Problems of the country under the Articles of Confederation

Congress didn't have any money.

There wasn't any President

The answers in the first three boxes are correct because they tell *three of the main problems* that the government had. But the answer in the fourth box is wrong. The selection doesn't say anything at all about the President. Include only the details from the selection in your answers.

NOTICE: Photocopying any part of this book is forbidden by law.

CORRECTING A PARAGRAPH

After you write something in your own words, it is important to **proofread your work**. This allows you to **correct mistakes** in spelling, punctuation, capitalization, and grammar. The third kind of short-answer question asks you to correct a writer's mistakes.

Read this example of a short-answer question.

Example 4

Here is a paragraph a student wrote about her vacation trip. The student made five mistakes in grammar, capitalization, and punctuation. Draw a line through each part that has a mistake and write the correction above it.

> Last summer my aunt took me to visit France
>
> for two weeks. We stayed with my ~~aunts~~ *aunt's* friend in a
>
> small town about thirty miles from ~~paris.~~ *Paris.* We went to
>
> see many museums and ~~churches we~~ *churches. We* ate at a lot of
>
> really great restaurants, too. But one of the things I
>
> liked best ~~were~~ *was* shopping for food. Instead of going to
>
> a supermarket, most French people like to shop at
>
> separate stores. First we went to a green grocer for
>
> ~~vegetable's.~~ *vegetables* Then we went to a butcher shop and a fish
>
> market. The best shop of all was a bakery. I'll never
>
> forget the delicious smell of fresh bread.

Note that all the corrections are clearly marked and neatly done. If you need to change an editing mark you've made on the test, that's fine. Just be sure to completely erase the mark that you don't want to appear.

NOTICE: Photocopying any part of this book is forbidden by law.

TIPS AND STRATEGIES
FOR WRITING SHORT ANSWERS TO
CONSTRUCTED-RESPONSE QUESTIONS

☞ Use your own words to answer constructed-response questions.

☞ Always read each question carefully to make sure you understand it.

☞ Always underline the **key words** in a question. This will help you stick to the topic in your answer.

☞ A question may have more than one part. Be sure you **answer all parts**.

☞ After writing your answer, check it over.

☞ When you use **complete sentences** to answer a question:

- Use key words from the question in your first sentence. Also include at least one story detail or fact that answers a part of the question.

- In the other few sentences, give other important details that help answer the question.

☞ When you **fill in a web or chart**:

- Be sure to read the text that is already on the web or chart. It will help you know what kinds of details belong in the empty places.

- Don't try to fill in the chart from memory. Check back in the selection to find the correct details.

☞ When you **correct a paragraph**:

- Proofread each sentence carefully.

- Mark the corrections neatly. If you want to change a correction, be sure to erase completely anything you don't want to appear.

SELECTIONS FOR PRACTICE

Selection 1

SAVING THE MOUNTAIN GORILLA

The mountain gorilla lives on the slopes of the Virungas, a range of volcanoes in eastern Africa. The gorillas were discovered by Western scientists in 1902. Over the next twenty-five years, hunters killed more than fifty of the rare animals. Meanwhile, the human population of East Africa kept growing and destroying much of the gorillas' habitat. The gorillas were forced into a smaller and smaller area. The increased contact with humans meant danger for another reason, too—disease. Gorillas can catch many diseases from humans, including measles, tuberculosis, influenza, and polio. These diseases can be deadly to gorillas.

By 1981 there were just 254 gorillas left. Today there are about 600, thanks mostly to the efforts of Dian Fossey. Scientist Dian Fossey began to study the gorillas in Rwanda in 1967. She alerted the world that the gorilla was in danger of extinction. But Fossey was mysteriously murdered in 1985. Some think she was killed by poachers who were angry at her efforts to keep them out of gorilla territory. Today, conservation groups continue her work.

1   **Write a few sentences to explain how mountain gorillas almost became extinct. Use details from the selection in your answer.**

_____

_____

_____

_____

_____

_____

    NOTICE: Photocopying any part of this book is forbidden by law.

Selection 2

PABLO PLANS A REPORT

P ablo decided to write a report about his town, Grantville. At first, he wasn't sure what to include. So first he did some research. He learned that the land for the town had been bought from the Lenni Lenape, the Native American people who used to live there. He decided to make the first part of the report about how they lived.

In the library, he learned how Grantville got its name. He would tell that in another part of his report. Then someone told him that Cornwall Hill was named for a family that once had a big farm on that road. He learned that some streets were named after other early settlers. He decided to make another part of the report about the early families who settled there.

In the town cemetery, Pablo saw that some graves had special markers showing that the men and women buried there had played a role in the Revolutionary War or the Civil War. He decided to make the last two parts of his report about the town during these two wars.

2 **Before he started writing, Pablo made this chart to show what each part of his report would tell. Fill in the rest of the boxes to show the parts of Pablo's report. Use details from the selection.**

Parts of Report	Information About Grantville
1	How the Lenni Lenape lived on the land before the settlers came
2	How Grantville got its name
3	
4	
5	

NOTICE: Photocopying any part of this book is forbidden by law.

Selection 3

 Here is a paragraph that a student wrote about kites. The student made five mistakes in grammar, capitalization, and punctuation. Draw a line through each part that has a mistake and write the correction above it.

Kite's have been around for a long time. They date back at least 2,000 years ago when the chinese made them from silk and bamboo. From China, kite flying spread to Japan during the sixth to the eighth centurys. The Japanese made kites in the forms of cranes dragons, fish, and turtles. Some of these animals brought good fortune and some was said to scare off evil spirits.

NOTICE: Photocopying any part of this book is forbidden by law.

19 WRITING LONG ANSWERS

GETTING THE IDEA

The test will ask you to write long answers to some questions. There are two kinds of **long-answer questions**:

1. One long-answer question will ask you to put ideas together from one or two selections and use your own words to write about them. You will need to use your reasoning power to **make decisions about what you have read**. For example:

   > **This article is about three English kings. How were the kings alike and how were they different? Use details from the article in your answer.**

   You will need to use details from the selection or selections to support what you say.

2. The second kind of long-answer question will also ask you to use your reasoning powers. But this kind of question will ask you to **express your own thoughts and feelings**. This means:

   - Give your opinion—what you think or feel about a story or topic.

   - Give your judgment—what you decide about an author's purpose or way of writing.

   - Connect ideas and experiences from the selection to your own life. For example, you might be asked to put yourself in a character's place and tell what you would do in the same situation. You might be asked to think of a real-life person who is like a character in a story. You might be asked how you might use the information you read about in your own life.

In this chapter, you will learn how to write long answers to constructed-response questions. The tips for success given in the short-answer chapter are also important for writing long answers. You'll discover more strategies as you learn about long-answer questions.

NOTICE: Photocopying any part of this book is forbidden by law.

151

PUTTING IDEAS TOGETHER

One kind of long-answer question will ask you to think about ideas from one or two selections and put them together in some way. You will be writing more than one paragraph to answer most questions. You don't have to fill every line on the page; but your answer does need to be organized, complete, and well written.

- **Organize your ideas**. As always, include key words from the question in the first sentence of your first paragraph. This helps you to focus on the topic. The other sentences in the first paragraph and following paragraphs should give details to support the topic, or main idea, sentence. Keep the details in each paragraph organized, too.

- **Use enough details**. Include as many as you need to give a complete answer. You can go back to the selection or selections whenever you need to find more details. You don't have to answer from memory.

- **Stick to the topic**. Make sure that all details you use in your paragraphs explain only the topic, or main idea, sentence.

- **Use connecting words**. Select the right words to show how ideas go together. You can use time words such as *first*, *next*, and *later*. You can use cause-and-effect words such as *because*, *since*, and *as a result*. You can use compare-and-contrast words such as *like*, *also*, *unlike*, and *however*.

- **Choose words carefully**. Select words that say exactly what you mean. Use verbs, adjectives, and adverbs that are clear and exact. This will help communicate your ideas well and make your writing more interesting.

The example on the next page asks you to put ideas together.

 NOTICE: Photocopying any part of this book is forbidden by law.

Example 1

The period from 800–1100 CE was known as the Viking Age. For about three hundred years, people in Europe lived in fear of surprise raids by the Vikings, or Norsemen. These fearless seamen came from Scandinavia, the area that is now the countries of Norway, Sweden, and Denmark.

During this period, the Vikings ruled the seas. Their ships were lighter and faster than anything known in the rest of Europe at the time. The Vikings could navigate the open sea, but their shallow-bottomed boats could also maneuver narrow rivers and lakes. With these boats they traveled farther than Europeans had ever gone before. They went to Russia and to southern France and Italy. They settled in northern France, where they became known as the Normans. They started settlements in Iceland and Greenland. They reached North America five hundred years before Columbus.

The Vikings also traded. They opened communication with people over great distances. They brought silks and spices from the Far East to Europe. They gave names to the places they settled, such as Greenland and Wicklow. Viking words such as *sister*, *outlaw*, and *skill* entered English and other languages. The Viking form of government influenced the places they settled and helped reshape the political structures of those countries. In fact, the effects of the Viking age are still being felt today.

1 **You read that the Vikings traveled further than Europeans had gone before and that they raided coastal settlements in Europe. Explain how the Vikings had a lasting influence on the world. Use details from the selection to support your answer.**

From 800–1100 CE, the Vikings sailed around the coast of Europe and had a lasting effect on the places they went. They raided, but they also they traded with people and started towns.

Because of their light, swift ships, the Vikings could travel farther than anyone else had gone. They brought back exotic spices from the Far East. They explored and settled new places such as Greenland and Iceland. They named places they went and the names are still used today. In addition, Viking words came into the languages of the places they went. The Vikings' type of government influenced the countries they settled, too.

NOTICE: Photocopying any part of this book is forbidden by law.

This is a very good answer to the question. Do you know why?

- ✓ The answer is organized. The topic, or main idea, sentence in the first paragraph uses the key words *Vikings* and *lasting effect* from the question. The other sentences in the first paragraph give details to support the main idea sentence. The writer chose and organized details that tell the ways the Vikings influenced the lands they reached.

- ✓ The next paragraph has a new main idea sentence that explains why the Vikings were able to travel far. It connects to the idea in the first paragraph. All the details in the second paragraph support the new main idea, and add more information about what the Vikings brought back from the places they visited.

- ✓ The answer sticks to the topic. The main idea sentence in the first paragraph says that the Vikings had a lasting effect on the places they went. The other details in the paragraph support only the main idea.

- ✓ The writer uses dates and connecting words such as *still* to show what happened over a period of time, and *in addition* to show connections between ideas.

- ✓ The writer uses adjectives such as *swift*, and *exotic* to give readers a clear picture of what was going on and to make the writing interesting.

Now read this example and question. Use the list above to help you write your answer to a question about the inventor of the ice cream cone.

Example 2

Who invented the ice cream cone? Some say it was Italo Marchiony. During the late 1890s, he sold lemon ices from a pushcart on Wall Street in New York City. When he ran out of dishes, he came up with the idea of making cones of pastry to hold the ices. Marchiony got a patent for his cone-making machine in 1903.

Some people say that the ice cream cone was invented in 1904 at the World's Fair in St. Louis. A Syrian immigrant named E. A. Hamwi had a pastry concession next to someone selling ice cream. When the ice cream vendors ran out of dishes, Hamwi rolled up some of his wafers, called Zalabia, into cones. He sold them to the ice cream vendors, and they became a huge hit.

NOTICE: Photocopying any part of this book is forbidden by law.

2   At least two men claimed to have invented the ice cream cone. Describe the claims and tell what is similar and different about each one. Use details from the selection to support your answer.

Your teacher will discuss your answer.

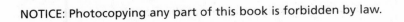

EXPRESSING YOUR OWN THOUGHTS AND FEELINGS

The second kind of long-answer question will ask you for your own thoughts and feelings about a topic. What you write can be quite different from what another person writes. However, you still need to present your thoughts and feelings clearly.

- **Organize your ideas**. As always, include key words from the question in your topic sentence. Remember that you will be giving your opinion or judgment, or you will be connecting something to your own life. So you can begin your topic sentence with phrases such as *I think, I feel, In my opinion, I would (or would not) enjoy* _____, *If I were* _____, and so on.

- **Stick to the topic**. The other sentences in your answer should give details to support or explain what you stated in your topic sentence.

- **Use connecting words**. You can use time words such as *first*, *next*, and *later* to tell something you would do. You can use cause-and-effect words such as *because*, *since*, and *as a result* to explain why you would or wouldn't enjoy something. You can use compare-and-contrast words such as *like*, *also*, *unlike*, and *however* to compare and contrast people and things in the selection to your own life.

- **Choose words carefully**. You should always write your thoughts and feelings clearly and make them interesting to read.

Here is an example that asks for an opinion. Read the selection about Jason, the main character. Then read the question and sample answer.

Example 3

Jason didn't know what else to do except to keep walking, following the road along the tracks. Train tracks always led somewhere, he reasoned. Even if they were rusty and no longer in use, they had to lead somewhere eventually. He hoped he'd chosen the right direction.

He wished now he hadn't slept while Pa was driving. When Pa got sick, he didn't know how far it was since they'd passed a town. He didn't know how far to the next one. They'd only seen one car coming from this way, early this morning.

NOTICE: Photocopying any part of this book is forbidden by law.

When Pa got sick, he'd made Jason drive, even though he was only fifteen. Jason had driven till they were almost out of gas. Then he pulled the truck over to the side of the road and parked in the shade of a big tree. He hadn't wanted to leave Pa alone. But then Pa passed out. He desperately needed help. Jason hoped he made the right decision to go for help. The road and the tracks had to lead somewhere, right? But would he find help in time?

3   **Do you think Jason was right to leave Pa alone to get help? Use details from the story to support your opinion.**

In my opinion, Jason made the right decision to leave Pa to get help. Waiting in the truck with him for help to come along wouldn't do any good. Since the place Jason had stopped the truck wasn't near a town, it seems clear that no one would suddenly appear to help. Since Jason had seen a car coming from the direction he was now walking, that was probably the best way to go. If he saw another car, he could flag it down for help.

This is a good answer. The writer stated an opinion in the topic sentence. The writer stayed with the topic and used details from the selection to support the opinion.

What is your opinion about Jason's decision? Write your thoughts and feelings on the lines below.

 Your teacher will discuss your answer.

_____

_____

_____

_____

_____

_____

NOTICE: Photocopying any part of this book is forbidden by law.

TIPS AND STRATEGIES
FOR WRITING LONG ANSWERS TO
CONSTRUCTED-RESPONSE QUESTIONS

☞ Remember that there are two kinds of **long-answer questions**. You will need to use your reasoning power to answer both kinds.

- One kind will ask you to **put ideas together** from one or two selections and **use your own words to write about them**.

- A second kind will ask you to **express your own thoughts and feelings**.

☞ When you put ideas together or write your thoughts and feelings:

- **Organize your ideas.** Include key words from the question in the first sentence of your first paragraph.

- **Use enough details.** Give as many as you need to give a complete answer. Go back to the selection or selections whenever you need to find more details. You don't have to answer from memory.

- **Stick to the topic.** Make sure that all details you use in your paragraphs explain the topic. Do not include details that have nothing to do with the topic.

- **Use connecting words.** Show how ideas go together by using time words, cause-and-effect words, and compare-and-contrast words.

- **Choose words carefully.** Use verbs, adjectives, and adverbs that are clear and exact.

☞ When you write your thoughts and feelings, remember that you can begin your topic sentence with phrases such as *I think*, *I feel*, *In my opinion*, *I would* (*or would not*) *enjoy* _____, *If I were* _____, and so on.

☞ Always proofread your writing. Check it for spelling, punctuation, capitalization, and grammar.

NOTICE: Photocopying any part of this book is forbidden by law.

SELECTIONS FOR PRACTICE

Selection 1

THE BIRTHDAY PRESENT

Rita woke up on Saturday feeling excited and grown up. It was her birthday! "I'm thirteen today!" she declared. "I'm a teenager."

Rita couldn't wait to see what her parents had bought her. She had been hinting for weeks about wanting a new CD player and speakers. She had already made room for the CD player by clearing off a shelf in her room, packing away her doll collection. She was too big for dolls now—even the expensive collectible ones that Mom had given her over the years.

Rita rushed downstairs. Mom probably had her present in the kitchen. She couldn't wait to play her new CDs!

"Happy Birthday, dear," said Mom and Dad together. "How's our little birthday girl?" Mom added.

Then they pointed to a large box in the dining room. Was it the CD player and speakers? Excitedly, Rita ripped off the paper. She held her breath.

Instead of the brown carton she expected, it was a large white box with a lid. With a sinking feeling, Rita lifted the lid and parted the tissue paper. There lay a large porcelain doll, dressed in a velvet coat. Rita felt her eyes fill with tears.

1   **Rita and her parents had different ideas about a present for her thirteenth birthday. Why do you think this misunderstanding happened? Use details from the story to explain your answer on the next page.**

NOTICE: Photocopying any part of this book is forbidden by law.

_____

_____

_____

_____

_____

_____

_____

_____

_____

_____

_____

_____

_____

_____

_____

_____

NOTICE: Photocopying any part of this book is forbidden by law.

Selection 2

LIFE IN THE MIDDLE AGES

When you think of the Middle Ages, you might imagine yourself as a knight, or perhaps a noble. But the odds are you would have been a peasant and lived a hard life.

The vast majority of peasants were poor farmers who worked land leased to them by the nobility. They lived in one- or two-room huts with a central fire. The huts had dirt floors and maybe a rough table and some stools. Peasants slept on a sack of straw.

The peasants were very isolated. There was, of course, no electricity and no telephone, telegraph, or radio. Nothing moved faster than a fast horse or swift ship. Most peasants lived their whole lives without ever traveling more than twenty or thirty miles from their home village.

If peasants didn't die in childhood and weren't killed off in an accident or by war, they lived to about 30 years of age. If they were sturdy and lucky, they might survive to "old age"—40 or 50. A rare few peasants made it to their 80s.

Perhaps the aspect of life then that is hardest for modern people to understand is the lack of privacy. People lived close together. Because there was no central heating, it was not uncommon in winter for a whole family to sleep in the same bed. Anyone who wanted to spend a lot of time alone was considered a little strange.

Today we are used to the idea that if you are smart and work hard, you can better yourself. You, or your child, might grow up to be President. But in the Middle Ages, your place in the social order was set. If you had been born a peasant, you, your children, and even your great-grandchildren would have been peasants, too.

2 **You have read about the life of a peasant in the Middle Ages. Write a paragraph or two to tell what you would like least about living as a peasant during this time. Use details from the selection to support your answer on the next page.**

NOTICE: Photocopying any part of this book is forbidden by law.

_____

_____

_____

_____

_____

_____

_____

_____

_____

_____

_____

_____

NOTICE: Photocopying any part of this book is forbidden by law.

PART 7: APPLYING EDITING SKILLS—LANGUAGE AND GRAMMAR

NOTICE: Photocopying any part of this book is forbidden by law.

20 PUNCTUATION AND CAPITALIZATION

Punctuation and capitalization are important elements of good, clear writing. This chapter will teach you how to do them correctly.

PUNCTUATION

Punctuation refers to the use of **end marks**, **commas**, and **apostrophes** to make the meaning of a sentence clear. Punctuation does for your writing what a change of voice or a pause does for speech.

END MARKS

An **end mark** goes at the end of a sentence. It shows where a complete thought stops.

(.) Use a period after most statements and commands.

Marco plays soccer every weekend. Give me the towel.

Use a period at the end of an abbreviation.

Dawan St.   Polecat, Inc.   Sat.

(!) The exclamation point is used after statements that show excitement or strong emotion.

We won!   Oh, no!   Hi!

(?) The question mark is used after a question.

Can you sing or dance?

NOTICE: Photocopying any part of this book is forbidden by law.

Example 1

1   **Which sentence has the correct punctuation?**

A   We can go to the zoo, but not to the beach?

B   Who will play the guitar at the party.

C   Watch out for the hole!

D   How did you do on the exam.

The correct answer choice is **C**. This statement shows strong emotions and excitement. It ends with an exclamation point. Choice A is a statement and should end with a period. Choices B and D should end with question marks.

Example 2

2   **Which sentence has the correct punctuation?**

A   Will you be able to come with us next week?

B   Please answer the phone?

C   Which hat do you want to wear.

D   Where is Smyth Street!

The correct answer choice is **A**. This sentence asks a question. It ends with a question mark. Choice B needs a period and choices C and D need a question mark.

NOTICE: Photocopying any part of this book is forbidden by law.

COMMAS

Use a **comma**:

- to separate three or more items in a series:

    We need some cheese, bread, mustard, and juice.

    It was a long, hard, dangerous hike.

- after an introductory word and after words that break the flow of thought in a sentence:

    Zach, you can ride with us. My friend Saidy, a great soccer player, has a knee injury.

- after a phrase that begins with a word or words such as *if, when, after, before, since, as a result:*

    If Usha and Marc can play, we'll have a great game.

    but NOT if it <u>ends</u> a sentence:

    We'll have a great game if Usha and Marc can play.

- to set off a direct quotation:

    "My dog hates going out in the rain," Rob said. "I'll walk Fuzzy in an hour," he added, "or when the rain stops."

- before *and*, *but*, *or*, and *yet* when they join two <u>complete</u> simple sentences into a compound sentence:

    Shana swims every day, and she also runs two miles.

- between the day and year in a date:

    July 4, 1776

    but NOT when <u>only</u> the month and the year are given:

    July 1776

- between the names of a city and state:

    Denver, Colorado

    and before and after the name of a state or country when it is used with the name of city in a sentence:

    They go to Nashville, Tennessee, every summer to see their grandparents.

NOTICE: Photocopying any part of this book is forbidden by law.

Example 3

3 **Which sentence does NOT use the comma correctly?**

A Jack will play the piano when Tamara and Raj sing.

B Senegalese food draws from native, French, Arabic, and Portuguese traditions.

C When Reba is sad her puppy always cheers her up.

D "You can go there tomorrow," Alan announced.

The correct answer choice is **C**. Use a comma after a phrase that starts with a word such as *if, when, after, before, since, as a result,* but only when the phrase begins a sentence. A comma should be added after *sad*.

Example 4

4 **Which sentence does NOT use the comma correctly?**

A Frank was born in Fargo, North Dakota.

B My great grandfather was born on July 4 1885.

C They've lived in Elkin Cove, Alaska, for ten years.

D Matt and Molly are the fastest runners, but Ahmed is the best pitcher.

The correct answer choice is **B**. Use a comma between the day and year in a date.

NOTICE: Photocopying any part of this book is forbidden by law.

APOSTROPHES

Use an **apostrophe**:

- to take the place of missing letters or numbers:

  They're going on a trip to Europe next month. (They are)

  I graduated from high school in '01. (2001)

- to show possession:

  an apostrophe and *s* ('s) to show one owner:

  Zaida's drawing   somebody's dog

  an apostrophe and *s* ('s) to show more than one owner when the plural noun does not end in *s*:

  people's choices   children's toys

  an apostrophe alone to show more than one owner when the plural noun ends in *s*:

  boys' teams   friends' houses

Special Rule!

- ✧ The words *it's* (with an apostrophe) means "it is." For example: It's not going to rain until Tuesday.

- ✧ The word *its* (NO apostrophe) means "belonging to it." For example: The raccoon washed its food before eating it.

        NOTICE: Photocopying any part of this book is forbidden by law.

Example 5

 5 **Which sentence does NOT use the apostrophe correctly?**

    A   The alligator's mouth snapped shut.

    B   It's humming kept me up all night.

    C   The children's skates were lined up in a row.

    D   Most of the boys' bats were made of wood.

Choice **B** does not use the apostrophe correctly. *It's* should be replaced by *its*—the possessive form.

Example 6

6 **Which sentence does NOT use the apostrophe correctly?**

    A   It's very simple to understand.

    B   The girls' coats are in the hall closet.

    C   The children's books are due back at the library.

    D   Theyll' take the bus to the mall.

Choice **D** does not use the apostrophe correctly. The contraction for *they will* is formed by leaving out the letters *wi* in *will*. So the apostrophe belongs before the *ll, they'll.*

NOTICE: Photocopying any part of this book is forbidden by law.

CAPITALIZATION

- The first word in a sentence always begins with a capital letter:

    This row is completely filled.

- The titles of movies, plays, and books begin with a capital letter:

    Around the World in Eighty Days

    The Music Man

- All words in titles are also capitalized except short words, such as the articles *a*, *an*, *the*; the short conjunctions *and*, *but*, *for*; and the short prepositions like *in*, *from*, *to*, *into*:

    Measure for Measure

    Alice in Wonderland

    America the Beautiful

- Proper nouns (names of companies, places, and holidays, for example) are always capitalized. In place names like *Atlantic Ocean* or *Amazon River*, both parts of the name are capitalized:

    Akron observes Memorial Day with a parade through the center of town.

- Titles such as *mayor*, *principal*, *aunt*, and *congresswoman* are capitalized when they appear before a name. Titles without a name are only capitalized when they belong to a high office holder:

    My aunt prefers to be called Professor Kimball.

    The President spoke to the Supreme Court about changing its decision.

NOTICE: Photocopying any part of this book is forbidden by law.

Example 7

7 **Which sentence does NOT use capitalization correctly?**

A   Jamie will go to Sherbrook High School next year.

B   The Museum of Fine Arts will show Monet's paintings in September.

C   Some businesses, like personal computers, inc., will offer discounts.

D   Aunt Martha is a pilot for Silver Wing Airlines.

Choice **C** does not use capitalization correctly. The company name should be capitalized: *Personal Computers, Inc.*

Example 8

8 **Which sentence does NOT use capitalization correctly?**

A   I'll meet you at Glenn lake in an hour.

B   Next February, Jana will compete in the Special Olympics.

C   Mike's mother is our principal.

D   The museum is located in Henry Horton State Park.

Choice **A** does not use capitalization correctly. In place names like *Glenn Lake*, both parts of the name are capitalized.

NOTICE: Photocopying any part of this book is forbidden by law.

QUICK PRACTICE

1 **Which sentence is NOT punctuated correctly?**

A Samuel dreamed of being an archeologist but his parents wanted him to be a dentist.

B The painter finished the child's portrait.

C Don't you want to sit in the back row?

D "Are you sure we're not lost?" Jennifer asked.

2 **Which sentence is NOT punctuated correctly?**

A The Santanas like to spend time in the town and in the country.

B They enjoy skiing sledding and skating in the winter.

C The family grows vegetables and herbs in the summer.

D When there's a full moon, you don't need a flashlight to see in the dark.

3 **Which sentence is NOT punctuated correctly?**

A The cat pounced on its prey.

B The women's whispers couldn't be heard.

C Birds beaks are usually very sharp.

D Three of the boys' uniforms were torn.

NOTICE: Photocopying any part of this book is forbidden by law.

4   **Which sentence is NOT punctuated correctly?**

A   The Sanchez family spends each summer in Puerto Rico.

B   Four bikes are parked in the Madisons' driveway.

C   What is this deserts' temperature at noon?

D   She was born on November 6, 2001.

5   **Which sentence is NOT punctuated correctly?**

A   If she wants to go tell her to call us.

B   Hannah sends all her letters by e-mail.

C   Can't we fit one more book in this backpack?

D   He's so glad you're here!

6   **Which sentence does NOT use capitalization correctly?**

A   My favorite trip is to the Museum of Natural History in New York City.

B   The Tennessee Titans would love to go to the Superbowl next year.

C   Carrie went to a dance on New Year's Eve.

D   The Longworth company is on Main avenue.

NOTICE: Photocopying any part of this book is forbidden by law.

GETTING THE IDEA

Grammar and Usage means choosing and using words carefully so that they say exactly what you mean. Correct grammar and usage means writing in a way that other people can understand: using nouns, verbs, adjectives, and adverbs that are clear and exact; and writing clear and complete sentences. Grammar and usage guides help you communicate your ideas well and make your writing more interesting.

SUBJECT-VERB AGREEMENT

When you write a sentence, make sure that the verb agrees with the subject. This means that they should both be singular or both be plural. In the present tense of most verbs, the endings change to agree with the subject.

- When the subject of a sentence is a **singular** noun, or the pronoun *he*, *she*, or *it*, use the verb form that ends in *s* or *es*.

    His friend plays soccer with my brother.

    She pitches a perfect game at least once in a season.

- When the subject of a sentence is **plural**, or the pronoun *I*, *we*, *you*, or *they*, do not add *s* or *es* to the verb.

    I read in the car.

    They listen carefully.

    People at sea watch and listen for storm warnings.

    Dogs chew shoes as well as bones.

    My friend's cats and our dogs like the same special treats.

Special Rule!

- Use the verb form that ends in *s* or *es* with the singular pronouns *everybody*, *everyone*, *everything*, *none*, *nobody*, *nothing*.

    Everybody brings something to the picnic.

    Everything seems fresh and new after the rain.

    Nothing bothers me when I sleep.

 NOTICE: Photocopying any part of this book is forbidden by law.

Example 1

1 **Which sentence has the incorrect verb form?**

A   Mr. Boris owns a dress shop.

B   Barry wants to volunteer with Habitat.

C   The clowns ride into the tent on horses.

D   Christina get a new dress for the party.

Choice **D** is the correct answer. *Christina* is the subject of the sentence and is singular. The sentence should read: *Christina gets a new dress for the party*.

Example 2

2 **Which sentence has the incorrect verb form?**

A   Drew wishes he could get new tires for his bike.

B   When our dog Pebbles is excited, she dash all around the room.

C   People want to have more than two choices on a menu.

D   None of the children is absent today.

Choice **B** is the correct answer. *She* is the subject of the sentence and is singular. The sentence should read: *She dashes all around the room*.

Example 3

3 **Which sentence has the incorrect verb form?**

A   Everybody usually skate on this playground.

B   Tonya fixes her own car most of the time.

C   Whenever he goes on vacation, he forgets something.

D   That group studies here every day.

Choice **A** is the correct answer. The special rule applies: Use the verb form that ends in *s* when the pronoun *everybody* is the subject of a sentence. The sentence should read: *Everybody usually skates on this playground*.

NOTICE: Photocopying any part of this book is forbidden by law.

QUICK PRACTICE

1   **Which sentence has the incorrect verb form?**

A   Not everyone likes to dance in the heat.

B   They have one more practice before the performance.

C   He visit his grandmother every Sunday afternoon.

D   When he walks, his shoes squeak.

2   **Which sentence has the incorrect verb form?**

A   All of the hamsters look healthy.

B   Who sing backup in your band?

C   Who takes the next turn with the weights?

D   All the dogs eat the same dry food.

3   **Which sentence has the incorrect verb form?**

A   He and Ling play flute and recorder.

B   The mango and the papaya are tropical fruits.

C   She always fixes her own bike.

D   Armin and Nicolai likes the same mystery stories.

   NOTICE: Photocopying any part of this book is forbidden by law.

PRONOUNS

A **pronoun** is a word that can be used in place of a noun.

A **subject pronoun** is a pronoun used as the subject of a sentence.

> I   you   he   she   it   we   they

> The boy has a hat collection. **He** started it when he was seven years old.

He is a pronoun that replaces the noun *boy*.

An **object pronoun** can be used as the **direct object of a verb**.

> me   you   him   her   it   us   them

> Aunt Rosa visited **them** last week.
> Marilyn asked Beverly and **him** to come to the swim meet.

HINT: There's a simple test for that last sentence. Try it without the words *Beverly and*: *Marilyn asked him to come to the swim meet.* (NOT *Marilyn asked he to come*)

An **object pronoun** can also be the **object of a preposition**. The object pronoun will come right after the preposition. Prepositions are words like *to, with, after,* and *for.*

> I handed the test to **her**. Zora waited for **them**.

Example 4

Read the following passage. Then answer the questions.

1
<u>Two</u> hundred years ago, Captains Meriwether Lewis and William Clark led

2   **3**
an expedition across the Louisiana Territory. Today, <u>we</u> know <u>it</u> as the

4
Northern Plains. <u>They</u> mapped their route and kept a journal. Historians

5   **6**
study <u>it</u> for details <u>about</u> these explorations. Sacagawea, a courageous Native

7   **8**   **9**
American woman <u>of</u> the Shoshone <u>nation</u>, helped the explorers. <u>She</u> located

10
horses and guides for <u>them</u>.

NOTICE: Photocopying any part of this book is forbidden by law.

4A   **Which word is NOT a pronoun used as a subject?**

   A   2

   B   1

   C   4

   D   9

The correct answer is Choice **B**. The word *two* is not a pronoun.

4B   **Which word is a pronoun used as the direct object of a verb?**

   A   6

   B   4

   C   5

   D   9

Choice **C** is correct. The word *about* (6) is a preposition; the words *they* (4) and *she* (9) are pronouns used as a subject.

4C   **Which word is a pronoun used as the object of a preposition?**

   A   3

   B   2

   C   7

   D   10

Choice **D** is correct. The word *them* is the object of the preposition *for*. The word *it* (3) is the direct object of the verb *know*; the word *we* (2) is a pronoun used as the subject of the sentence; the word *of* (7) is a preposition, not a pronoun.

NOTICE: Photocopying any part of this book is forbidden by law.

QUICK PRACTICE

Four of these sentences have personal pronouns used incorrectly. Draw a line through each part that has a mistake, and write the correction above it.

1. He asked Erik and I to try out for the play.

2. Her and Keisha are the tallest players on the team.

3. May him and me come to the movie, too?

4. Coach Haro will be with us for only one more season.

5. Mrs. Michaels and us can show you around.

VERBS

A **verb** is a word that shows action:

> They **practice** every Tuesday.

A verb can also show a state of being:

> They **are** happy.

When you write about something **happening now**, use the **present tense** of the verb:

> Marty **handles** the elephants well. He **begins** by talking to them.

When you write about something that **has happened**, use the **past tense** of the verb:

> Marty **handled** the elephants well during last week's storm.

> He **began** by talking to them in a comforting voice.

When you write about something that **will happen**, use the **future tense** of the verb:

> Next year we **will go** to a new school.

Most verbs form the past tense by adding *ed*. **Irregular verbs** do not:

> They **ran** four miles yesterday.

> Last week, my brother **rode** his bike across town.

Some verbs have a special spelling when used with the helping verbs *have*, *has*, or *had*:

> They **have run** this far many times.

> He **has ridden** across town many times.

 NOTICE: Photocopying any part of this book is forbidden by law.

Here are some of the common irregular verbs:

SOME COMMON IRREGULAR VERBS

Present	Past	Past Participle
am	was	(have) been
are	were	(have) been
begin	began	(have) begun
blow	blew	(have) blown
bring	brought	(have) brought
choose	chose	(have) chosen
come	came	(have) come
do	did	(have) done
draw	drew	(have) drawn
drink	drank	(have) drunk
drive	drove	(have) driven
eat	ate	(have) eaten
fall	fell	(have) fallen
freeze	froze	(have) frozen
give	gave	(have) given
go	went	(have) gone
has	had	(have) had

Present	Past	Past Participle
hide	hid	(have) hidden
is	was	(have) been
leave	left	(have) left
let	let	(have) let
lose	lost	(have) lost
run	ran	(have) run
see	saw	(have) seen
sink	sank	(have) sunk
speak	spoke	(have) spoken
swing	swung	(have) swung
take	took	(have) taken
tell	told	(have) told
think	thought	(have) thought
throw	threw	(have) thrown
wear	wore	(have) worn
win	won	(have) won
write	wrote	(have) written

NOTICE: Photocopying any part of this book is forbidden by law.

181

Example 5

5 **Which of these sentences uses the correct verb form?**

A Becky has went to the rodeo.

B It was so cold that my lunch had froze.

C You have drove there many times.

D I gave her my last quarter.

Choice **D** is correct. The verb form in sentence A should be *has gone*. The verb form in sentence B should be *had frozen*. The verb form in sentence C should be *have driven*. Substitute the correct forms and reread the sentences.

Example 6

6 **Which of these sentences uses the correct verb form?**

A The guests drunk everything in the first hour of the party.

B Yesterday the wind blowed part of our roof off.

C The American flag flew proudly in every public place across the country.

D In last Saturday's game, the quarterback run the wrong way with the ball.

Choice **C** is correct. The correct verb form in sentence A is *drank*. The correct verb form in sentence B is *blew*. The correct verb form in sentence D is *ran*. Substitute the correct forms and reread the sentences.

NOTICE: Photocopying any part of this book is forbidden by law.

Example 7

7 **Which of these sentences uses the correct verb form?**

A   Smitty drank more water than all the other hikers.

B   Matt had chose his costume early.

C   Bill and Joe been fishing there many times.

D   I worn the same socks for two days.

Choice **A** is correct. The past form of the verb *drink* is *drank*. The correct verb form in sentence B should be *had chosen*. The correct verb form in sentence C should be *had been fishing* or *have been fishing*. The correct verb form in sentence D should be *wore* or *have worn*.

Example 8

8 **Which of these sentences uses the correct verb form?**

A   The whole class has wrote good reports.

B   Yesterday they done their homework late.

C   Linda spoken to her coach yesterday.

D   The parents had hidden the presents in the closet.

Choice **D** is correct. The past participle of *hide* is *had hidden*. The correct verb form in sentence A is *has written*. The correct verb form in sentence B is *did*. The correct verb form in sentence C is *had spoken*.

QUICK PRACTICE

Four of these sentences have verb forms that are used incorrectly. Draw a line through each part that has a mistake, and write the correction above it.

1. Have you chose what classes you will take next year?

2. The batter swing and missed three pitches.

3. When the band begun to play, students sang "America the Beautiful."

4. Do you remember what you worn to the last school dance?

5. A fierce wind had blown the roof off the gym.

NOTICE: Photocopying any part of this book is forbidden by law.

22 SPELLING

You can improve your spelling by using a dictionary, learning words your teacher gives you, and most of all, by reading. The more you read, the more words you will see spelled correctly.

Many words sound the same or similar but are spelled differently and have different meanings. Below is a list of commonly confused word pairs. Learn the correct spelling and meaning of these words.

accept (to receive)
except (other than; leaving out)

> We cannot **accept** your terms.
> They sold everything **except** the coffee table.

access (approach to places, things, or people)
excess (the part that is too much)

> Only reporters can gain **access** backstage.
> They donated their **excess** supplies to the school.

advice (opinion about what should be done)
advise (to inform; to give advice to)

> I need **advice** on the situation.
> I **advise** you to get a lawyer.

affect (to produce a result on; to touch or influence)
effect (the result)

> Lack of time can **affect** your work.
> You can still see the **effect** of the hurricane.

all ready (completely prepared)
already (by this time)

> Are you **all ready** for your vacation?
> Aaron and Jonathan have finished their homework **already**.

NOTICE: Photocopying any part of this book is forbidden by law.

brake (anything used to slow or stop moving wheels)
break (damage; to make something come apart)

>The **brake** needs repair.
>Don't **break** the vase!

capital (city where the government of a state or country is located)
capitol (the building where the U.S. Congress or the state legislature meets)

>Nashville is the **capital** of Tennessee.
>The state assembly is in the **capitol** building.

desert (a sandy region without water and trees)
dessert (the last course of a meal)

>The **desert** sun baked the sand under his feet.
>My favorite **dessert** is vanilla ice cream.

fair (giving the same treatment to all; according to the rules;
   in a just way; average)
fare (money paid for transportation)

>The players said the new rule wasn't **fair**.
>Did you pay your train **fare**?

farther (a distance that can be measured)
further (more; more distant)

>The library is **farther** away than the bookstore.
>We're waiting for **further** information about the meteor shower.
>Despite their efforts, they grew **further** apart.

hear (take in sounds through the ear; listen)
here (in this place; at this place; to this place)

>Do you **hear** the ocean?
>The teacher is not **here** today.

it's (it is)
its (belonging to it)

>**It's** a large, grey cat.
>**Its** paws look like little white socks.

NOTICE: Photocopying any part of this book is forbidden by law.

led (past form of the verb *to lead*: to show the way)
lead (a heavy, easily melted metal)

> The largest elephant **led** the parade.
> The **lead** pipes were stacked in a pile.

loose (free, not contained)
lose (not have any longer; fail to get; have taken away by accident or carelessness)

> The dress was too **loose** on her.
> I **lose** my gloves all the time.

past (time gone by, ended; beyond)
passed (went by; went from person-to-person; got through)

> In the **past**, women were not allowed to vote.
> As time **passed**, their efforts paid off, and they won the right to vote.

peace (quiet, calm; freedom from fighting)
piece (one part of something)

> After a noisy morning, Carl wanted some **peace** and quiet.
> Can I have a **piece** of that cake?

principal (main, chief, most important; the head of a school; one who gives orders)
principle (basic truth or law; rule of action or conduct; high standard of behavior)

> The **principal** established new rules of conduct.
> We learned a new **principle** in science.

stationary (having a fixed place; unable to move)
stationery (writing material such as paper, cards, envelopes)

> Those seats are **stationary**.
> Erin always wrote letters on her own **stationery**.

than (in comparison with)
then (at that time; after that)

> Mia is taller **than** her sister, Faye.
> Do your homework, **then** you can play outside.

NOTICE: Photocopying any part of this book is forbidden by law.

their (shows ownership)
there (in or at that place; word used to introduce a sentence)
they're (contraction for *they are*)

Their pet turtle kept trying to run away.

Macy is standing over **there**.

They're running in the race this Saturday.

threw (tossed; brought to the ground)
through (from end to end of; between the parts of)

The pitcher **threw** the ball.

The ball went **through** the window.

to (a preposition showing motion toward)
too (also)
two (a number)

Julissa went **to** her ballet class right after school.

We're going to the game. Will you come, **too**?

Do you see **two** cats up in that tree?

waste (make poor use of; fail to get the most out of something)
waist (the part of the body between the ribs and the hips)

Water is too valuable to **waste**.

He wore a fancy leather belt around his **waist**.

weather (condition of the air at a certain place and time)
whether (word used in expressing choices)

She listened carefully to the **weather** report.

James hasn't decided **whether** to go or not.

whose (shows ownership)
who's (contraction for *who is*)

Whose jacket was left in the closet?

Who's interested in volunteering?

 NOTICE: Photocopying any part of this book is forbidden by law.

Read each sentence and decide which word is spelled incorrectly. If all the words in a sentence are spelled correctly, choose D.

Example 1

    A   **B**   **C**

<u>Whose</u> making <u>dessert</u> for dinner? If you want my <u>advice</u>, have Sam make it.

A   *Whose* should be written *Who's*.

B   *Dessert* should be written *desert*.

C   *Advice* should be written *advise*.

D   Make no change.

Think about the two words that sound alike, but have different meanings and different spellings. Which of the two fits the meaning in the sentence? Choice **A** is correct. *Who's* is the contraction for *Who is*.

Example 2

    A   **B**   **C**

<u>There</u> are <u>two</u> misspelled words on that <u>peace</u> of paper.

A   *There* should be written *Their*.

B   *Two* should be written *to*.

C   *Peace* should be written *piece*.

D   Make no change.

Think about the two words that sound alike, but have different meanings and different spellings. Which of the two fits the meaning in the sentence? Choice **C** is correct. *Piece* means "part of something," as in a piece of paper.

NOTICE: Photocopying any part of this book is forbidden by law.

Example 3

                 A   **B**

The snowy <u>weather</u> caused many problems in the <u>past</u> two weeks. So the

C

<u>principle</u> closed school early.

      A   *Weather* should be written *whether*.

      B   *Past* should be written *passed*.

      C   *Principle* should be written *principal*.

      D   Make no change.

Think about the two words that sound alike, but have different meanings and different spellings. Which of the two fits the meaning in the sentence? Choice **C** is correct. *Principal* means "the head of a school; one who gives orders."

Example 4

     A   **B**   **C**

<u>It's</u> important to get <u>they're</u> votes on raising the bus <u>fare</u>.

      A   *It's* should be written *Its*.

      B   *They're* should be written *their*.

      C   *Fare* should be written *fair*.

      D   Make no change.

Think about the two words that sound alike, but have different meanings and different spellings. Which of the two fits the meaning in the sentence? Choice **B** is correct. *Their* shows ownership.

 NOTICE: Photocopying any part of this book is forbidden by law.

QUICK PRACTICE

Read each sentence and decide which word is spelled incorrectly. If all the words in a sentence are spelled correctly, choose D.

1

                          A   **B**

A big snowstorm was about to <u>break</u>; but that did not <u>affect</u> the hikers.

              C

They were <u>already</u> for lots of snow.

A   *Break* should be written *brake*.

B   *Affect* should be written *effect*.

C   *Already* should be written *all ready*.

D   Make no change.

2

                    A   **B**

They had <u>access</u> to a large cabin; but they didn't want to <u>loose</u> any time.

                    C

So they walked right <u>past</u> it.

A   *Access* should be written *excess*.

B   *Loose* should be written *lose*.

C   *Past* should be written *passed*.

D   Make no change.

3

  A   **B**

<u>Their</u> camp was only five miles <u>farther</u>; but they knew the trip would

                C

take longer <u>then</u> usual because of the weather.

A   *Their* should be written *There*.

B   *Farther* should be written *further*.

C   *Then* should be written *than*.

D   Make no change.

NOTICE: Photocopying any part of this book is forbidden by law.

A   **B**

The guide <u>threw</u> snowballs as he <u>lead</u> them forward. Everyone could

C

have some fun as long as they didn't <u>lose</u> their way.

A   *Threw* should be written *through*.

B   *Lead* should be written *led*.

C   *Lose* should be written *loose*.

D   Make no change.

A   **B**

Everyone, <u>except</u> the guide, was so tired that they didn't eat <u>dessert</u>.

C

<u>Whose</u> going to eat it now?

A   *Except* should be written *accept*.

B   *Dessert* should be written *desert*.

C   *Whose* should be written *Who's*.

D   Make no change.

NOTICE: Photocopying any part of this book is forbidden by law.

23 SENTENCE STRUCTURE

In this chapter you will learn how to correct run-on sentences and sentence fragments (incomplete sentences). You will also learn how to combine sentences that are too short and choppy.

RUN-ON SENTENCES

People often make the mistake of writing two sentences as one. This creates confusion for the reader. Where does one sentence end and the next one begin? This kind of sentence is called a **run-on**. Here are two examples of run-ons. The first example uses a comma between two main clauses (complete sentences); the second example does not.

> The team wanted to keep practicing, the coach made them stop.

> The team wanted to keep practicing the coach made them stop.

You have three ways to correct a run-on:

1. Make two sentences. Put a period or other end mark after the first main clause. Start the new sentence with a capital letter:

   > The team wanted to keep practicing. The coach made them stop.

2. Put a semicolon after the first main clause. Semicolons are most effective when the ideas are very closely connected.

   > The team wanted to keep practicing; the coach made them stop.

3. Add a coordinating conjunction such as *and, or, but*, or *yet*. Put a comma before the conjunction.

   > The team wanted to keep practicing, but the coach made them stop.

NOTICE: Photocopying any part of this book is forbidden by law.

Example 1

The year was 1879 explorers made an amazing discovery in Spain. On the walls of a cave in Spain were some beautiful paintings. Some scientists thought they were painted during the Stone Age, between ten and thirty thousand years ago. Special tests proved that these scientists were correct, and explorers continued their search for other examples.

1 **Which sentence is a run-on?**

    A   1

    B   2

    C   3

    D   4

The correct answer is Choice **A**. This run-on sentence should be broken into two separate sentences as follows: *The year was 1879. Explorers made an amazing discovery in Spain.*

NOTICE: Photocopying any part of this book is forbidden by law.

Example 2

▼¹ Cave paintings have also been found in France, Spain, Italy, and Russia. ▼² The first humans lived in Africa and the Middle East scientists believe they will find more cave paintings in these parts of the world. ▼³ Many paintings are close to cave entrances; the painters needed sunlight to see what they were doing. ▼⁴ Some paintings have been found deep inside caves, and scientists have seen hints that the artists used torches as light sources.

2 **Which sentence is a run-on?**

A   1
B   2
C   3
D   4

The correct answer is Choice **B**. This run-on sentence should be broken into two separate sentences as follows: *The first humans lived in Africa and the Middle East. Scientists believe they will find more cave paintings in these parts of the world.*

NOTICE: Photocopying any part of this book is forbidden by law.

SENTENCE FRAGMENTS

The test may ask you to identify or fix **sentence fragments**—sometimes called incomplete sentences. A complete sentence must contain a **subject** and a **predicate**. The predicate is the part of the sentence that contains the **verb**. It must express a complete thought. Here are some examples of complete sentences:

> The train arrived at the station on time.

> The play was more fun than he had imagined.

> Our family eats dinner precisely at seven.

Now look at some sentence fragments:

> Quickly down the hall.

> Ran into the house.

> A tall woman in a blue dress.

None of these fragments has a subject and a verb. *Who* moved quickly down the hall or ran into the house? *What action* did the tall woman take? So none of them should end with a period. Some need a subject, or a verb, or both:

> They walked quickly down the hall. (needed subject and predicate)

> The dog ran into the house. (needed a subject)

> A tall woman in a blue dress played the trombone. (needed a predicate)

Another very common kind of sentence fragment begins with words like *after*, *before*, *because*, *since*, and *when*.

> Since the day before yesterday.

> Before I could catch it.

Both of these examples need both a subject and predicate either at the beginning or at the end.

> I have been ill since the day before yesterday.

> Before I could catch it, the glass fell to the floor.

 NOTICE: Photocopying any part of this book is forbidden by law.

Try the examples below and on the next page. Remember that a complete sentence must have a subject and a predicate. It should express a complete thought on its own, without depending on the sentences that precede or follow it.

Example 3

▼¹There was a fire on the Villanovas' farm. ▼²When they were away on vacation. ▼³A large, empty barn burned down. ▼⁴Because no one saw the blaze, the fire department was not called in time.

3 **Which sentence in this passage is a fragment?**

    A   1

    B   2

    C   3

    D   4

Choice **B** is the sentence fragment. It should be joined to the first sentence: *There was a fire on the Villanova's farm when they were away on vacation.*

NOTICE: Photocopying any part of this book is forbidden by law.

Example 4

[1] The modern steam engine was invented in 1769 by Scottish engineer and inventor James Watt. [2] In 1804, an American inventor named Oliver Evans said he could create a steam carriage that would run 15 miles an hour. [3] On level railways. [4] Then, in 1812, Colonel John Stevens of Hoboken, New Jersey, began to envision a railway that would link distant sections of the nation. [5] The railroad finally had a far-reaching effect on the way people and goods were transported.

4 **Which sentence in this passage is incomplete?**

A 1

B 2

C 3

D 5

Choice **C** is the incomplete sentence. It should be joined to the sentence before it: *In 1804, an American inventor named Oliver Evans said he could create a steam carriage that would run 15 miles an hour on level railways.*

NOTICE: Photocopying any part of this book is forbidden by law.

COMBINING SENTENCES

Sometimes it is a good idea to combine two short sentences into a longer one.

Short sentences:

> The hikers had been climbing hills all morning.

> They were feeling very tired.

Here are some ways to combine two short, choppy sentences into one sentence:

You can place a comma followed by a conjunction, such as *or*, *and*, or *but*, where the period used to be. Be sure that there is a complete sentence before and after the conjunction. If there is not, then add the conjunction but no comma.

> The hikers had been climbing hills all morning, and they were feeling very tired.

You can join two sentences with a joining word that supports the meaning of the sentence. Words like *although*, *after*, *before*, *since*, or *because* are useful joining words.

> Because the hikers had been climbing hills all morning, they were feeling very tired.

Sometimes, you can place a semicolon where the period used to be:

> The hikers had been climbing hills all morning; they were feeling very tired.

Notice that you should NOT join two sentences by commas alone. You would create a run-on. The following sentence would be incorrect:

INCORRECT:

> The hikers had been climbing hills all morning, they were feeling tired.

NOTICE: Photocopying any part of this book is forbidden by law.

199

Read the following sentences and decide on the best way to combine them.

Example 5

Bryan was at the bus stop early. The school bus was late.

5 **What is the best way to combine these two sentences?**

A Bryan was at the bus stop early, the school bus was late.

B Because Bryan was at the bus stop early, the school bus was late.

C Bryan was at the bus stop early, but the school bus was late.

D The school bus was late after Bryan was at the bus stop early.

Choice **C** is the best answer. The word *but* shows that the two events were opposites: Bryan was early, **but** the bus was late. Choice A is incorrect because you can't join two sentences with only a comma. Choice B is incorrect, since the combining word *because* changes the meaning of the sentence. Choice D uses the wrong word to join the two sentences, and the meaning changes. Another way to write it correctly would be: *The school bus was late, although Bryan was at the bus stop early.*

Example 6

We heard loud thunder from the west. We thought it might rain.

6 **What is the best way to combine these sentences without changing their meaning?**

A Although we heard loud thunder from the west, we thought it might rain.

B We heard loud thunder from the west because we thought it might rain.

C We heard loud thunder from the west, we thought it might rain.

D We heard loud thunder from the west, so we thought it might rain.

Choice **D** is the best answer. It uses a comma and a joining word that does not change the meaning of the sentence. Choice A is incorrect because the combining word *although* changes the meaning, and doesn't make sense. Choice B is incorrect. The combining word *because* changes the meaning of the sentence. Choice C is incorrect because you can't join two sentences with only a comma.

 NOTICE: Photocopying any part of this book is forbidden by law.

QUICK PRACTICE

Selection 1

Marc wrote a report about Walt Disney. This is part of his rough draft. Read it, and do the questions that follow.

▼¹Not every child in the twentieth century could view animated cartoons. ▼²Didn't exist until the late 1920s. ▼³At that time, cartoonist Walt Disney tried a new technology, the moving picture. ▼⁴The moving picture made his characters seem to move. ▼⁵Mickey Mouse was the first cartoon character to have a sound track he was first named Mortimer Mouse.

1A **Which sentence is a run-on?**

A   2

B   3

C   5

D   1

1B **Which sentence is a fragment?**

A   2

B   3

C   4

D   5

1C **Which two sentences should be combined?**

A   2 and 3

B   3 and 4

C   4 and 5

D   None should be combined.

NOTICE: Photocopying any part of this book is forbidden by law.

Selection 2

This report about Buffalo Bill Cody can stand some improvement. Read it, and do the questions that follow.

▼[1] "Buffalo Bill" was the nickname of William Cody. ▼[2] He led an exciting life during the days of the Wild West. ▼[3] He was a rider for the Pony Express. ▼[4] At the age of fifteen. ▼[5] During the Civil War, he was a scout for the Union forces. ▼[6] Buffalo Bill got his name when he supplied buffalo meat to the workers building a railroad west through Kansas. ▼[7] His most successful career was as a showman. ▼[8] He put together "Wild West" shows that played all over the United States and parts of Europe. ▼[9] In these shows, Buffalo Bill often played himself, and recounted his adventures, and even appeared in silent films before he died in 1917.

2A **What is the best way to combine Sentences 1 and 2 without changing their meaning?**

A "Buffalo Bill" was the nickname of William Cody, who led an exciting life during the days of the Wild West.

B "Buffalo Bill" was the nickname of William Cody, he led an exciting life during the days of the Wild West.

C "Buffalo Bill" was the nickname of William Cody, but he led an exciting life during the days of the Wild West.

D "Buffalo Bill" was the nickname of William Cody, so he led an exciting life during the days of the Wild West.

 NOTICE: Photocopying any part of this book is forbidden by law.

2B   **Which sentence is NOT complete?**

A   3

B   4

C   7

D   9

2C   **Which is the best way to correct Sentence 9?**

A   In these shows, Buffalo Bill often played himself, recounted his adventures, even appeared in silent films before he died in 1917.

B   In these shows, Buffalo Bill often played himself, although he recounted his adventures, and even appeared in silent films before he died in 1917.

C   In these shows, Buffalo Bill often played himself, and recounted his adventures because he appeared in silent films before he died in 1917.

D   In these shows, Buffalo Bill often played himself and recounted his adventures. He even appeared in silent films before he died in 1917.

PART 8: PRACTICE TEST

SPACE, THE FINAL FRONTIER

Space exploration continues to intrigue us. There is a vast universe beyond our reach, and we have more questions than answers. Nonetheless, we have made great progress in answering those questions. With improved technology, we forge ahead, learning more about the universe we are a part of.

NOTICE: Photocopying any part of this book is forbidden by law.

TIPS FOR TAKING THE TEST

Before you start the Practice Test, here are some good tips:

1. Relax.

2. Read the directions before you answer the questions. Ask your teacher to explain any directions you do not understand.

3. Read each question carefully. Read all the answer choices. Choose the best answer; but don't guess. You may look back at the reading selection when needed.

4. Look for important words in the questions. Key words like *best*, *not*, *same as*, and *different* tell you what to look for.

5. Don't spend too long on one question.

6. Try to answer all the test questions.

7. When you write your answers, be sure to include details from the reading selection to support or explain your answer.

   Your writing WILL BE scored on:

   • how clearly you organize and express your ideas

   • how accurately and completely you answer the questions

   • how well you support your ideas with examples

   • how interesting and enjoyable your writing is to read

   • how correctly you use grammar, spelling, punctuation, and capitalization

STOP: Wait for your teacher's instructions before beginning the Practice Test.

NOTICE: Photocopying any part of this book is forbidden by law.

Directions

This is a biography of astronaut Cady Coleman. Read the selection. Then answer Numbers 1 through 8.

From Student to
ASTRONAUT

Catherine G. "Cady" Coleman's journey to becoming a NASA astronaut began in high school. Mrs. Ruth Opp, an enthusiastic teacher, turned her on to science. "She passed her excitement on to me," Coleman says. "She made me want to know more about chemistry." So Coleman studied chemistry in college.

Coleman didn't even think about becoming an astronaut until one day when she attended a talk by a special speaker—Sally Ride. Ride was the first American woman in space.

Coleman was inspired. "I thought, wow, I want that job! I wanted adventure in my life."

So after college, Coleman joined the Air Force, and eventually earned a doctorate degree in chemistry. Meantime, she applied for the astronaut program. Then, in 1992, her dream came true when NASA chose her to become an astronaut. The next step was NASA's "basic training school." There she learned how the space shuttle works and how to be a space shuttle operator.

Every astronaut is first a scientist. One of the most important things they do on the space shuttle is conduct experiments in the low-gravity lab. Here they grow plants, or work to discover how substances behave—all in the low gravity of space. When Coleman joined NASA, she didn't stop doing science. But her involvement shifted from doing her own research to helping other scientists develop the experiments that would be done on the shuttle.

Go On

NOTICE: Photocopying any part of this book is forbidden by law.

207

Because shuttle trips are short--only 16 days—every moment counts. Each experiment is worked out carefully beforehand. The astronauts begin training to conduct the research about two years before a flight. They must understand the purpose of each experiment thoroughly, and learn how to adapt it to space. That way, if changes have to be made during the flight, the astronauts can keep the original goal in mind.

Coleman flew her first space mission on board the shuttle *Columbia* in 1995, working on the US Microgravity Laboratory (USML-2). During her 16-day flight, Coleman conducted experiments, many of which involved how liquids behave in space under low gravity.

In 1999, Coleman flew again, as part of the shuttle mission which launched the Chandra X-Ray telescope into space. "During the Chandra mission," Coleman said, "I started to fill in the holes in my head where astronomy is supposed to live."

Coleman now works in Mission Control. She is the person the astronauts speak with when they call home. Her experience in space and as a scientist comes in handy here, too. She knows there must be a balance between maintaining communication with the astronauts and giving them time to complete their tasks. As she communicates with the astronauts, she is getting a bird's eye view of what it is like to live and work in space for a longer time. "I can't tell you," she says, "how much it makes me want to go back!"

Coleman looks forward to working one day on the International Space Station. While shuttle flights are only about 16 days long, scientists working on the space station remain in space for several months at a time. Experiments can be done leisurely, and there is time for more scientific exploration. "So much of science is in the mistakes and being aware and intelligent enough to observe them and then learn from them," said Coleman.

In the meantime, she keeps learning. "That's one of the reasons that I love my job," she says. "Every day and every mission is a little different, but they have one thing in common—I am always learning something."

NOTICE: Photocopying any part of this book is forbidden by law.

1   Here is a timeline of some important events in Cady Coleman's life.

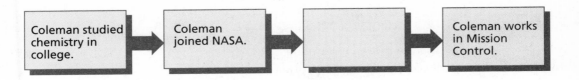

Coleman studied chemistry in college. → Coleman joined NASA. → [ ] → Coleman works in Mission Control.

What belongs in the empty box?

A   Coleman studied chemistry in high school.

B   Coleman joined the Air Force.

C   Coleman heard Sally Ride speak.

D   Coleman flew on space shuttle *Columbia*.

2   Which of the following statements is NOT true of astronaut Cady Coleman?

F   She earned a degree in chemistry.

G   She was inspired by Sally Ride.

H   As a small child, she wanted to be an astronaut.

J   She conducted experiments in space.

3   Coleman said, "I started to fill in the holes in my head where astronomy is supposed to live." Which sentence best explains what she meant?

A   Coleman had holes in her head.

B   Astronomy explains where holes live.

C   Coleman was not interested in astronomy.

D   Coleman began to learn about astronomy.

Go On

NOTICE: Photocopying any part of this book is forbidden by law.

4   **This article is mostly about**

    F   being a chemist

    G   the importance of great teachers

    H   an astronaut's training and work

    J   flying on space shuttles

5   **Based on the information in this passage, what will Coleman probably do?**

    A   Coleman will stay with NASA.

    B   Coleman will leave NASA.

    C   Coleman will become a pilot.

    D   Coleman will become a chemistry teacher.

6   **The article mentions two people who inspired Cady Coleman. Name the two people and explain how each influenced her.**

_____

_____

_____

_____

NOTICE: Photocopying any part of this book is forbidden by law.

7 Coleman's present job is to be the ground person who communicates with the astronauts during their flight. How do Coleman's education, training, and experiences make her a good person for this job? Use information from the article to support your answer.

_____

_____

_____

_____

_____

_____

_____

_____

_____

_____

_____

_____

_____

Go On

NOTICE: Photocopying any part of this book is forbidden by law.

8 Has someone in your life inspired you to do something? Or have you inspired someone else in some way? Tell about this person and the circumstances.

You might write about someone you admire, even if the person has not inspired you to actually do something. Be sure to tell why you admire this person.

_____

_____

_____

_____

_____

_____

_____

NOTICE: Photocopying any part of this book is forbidden by law.

Directions

People have long been fascinated by Mars. A lot is known about it, and yet there is so much more to learn. Read the following article about Mars. Then answer Numbers 9 through 16.

Could There Be Life on MARS?

Most scientists are convinced that life exists on other planets, somewhere in the universe. Could it be on Mars?

Two requirements for life on any planet are water and a moderate climate. Mars doesn't seem to have either. The red planet is very dry. Martian air contains only about 1/1,000 as much water as our air. Although thin ice clouds form, there is not enough moisture for rain to fall. So there are no oceans, lakes, or rivers on the surface of Mars.

The climate on Mars is not friendly either. Mars is much colder than Earth. The average temperature is a frigid −67° Fahrenheit (−55° C). But even worse, conditions change quickly. One day it will be a warm (by Martian standards) -40° F and there will be planet-wide dust storms. Then suddenly, the temperature drops 40° and the entire planet is covered with ice clouds!

One reason for this quickly changing climate is that Mars' orbit is shaped like an ellipse, or oval. This means that sometimes Mars is much closer to the Sun than it is at other times. So there is a great variation in how much sunlight and heat Mars receives.

Another reason the climate changes quickly is Mars' thin atmosphere. On Earth, the thick atmosphere acts like a blanket to keep temperatures moderate. Also, Earth's oceans absorb and hold the sun's heat. But Mars' atmosphere is paper-thin (about 1/100th as thick as Earth's) and makes a poor blanket. In addition, there are no oceans on Mars to store up and give back heat from the sun. So temperatures on Mars shift dramatically from day to night and from season to season. Life on Mars would have to be able to adapt to these roller coaster conditions.

Go On

NOTICE: Photocopying any part of this book is forbidden by law.

There's another problem on Mars: radiation. The thin Martian atmosphere lets almost all of the sun's radiation through. The radiation on Mars is strong enough to wipe out all life on the planet.

Yet, despite the dryness, cold, and radiation, Mars is still the most Earth-like of the planets in our solar system. Its day is about the same length as ours. It has polar ice caps and seasons. And compared to the other planets in our solar system, the temperature is not *that* extreme. (Venus, for example, has a surface temperature of 872.4° F, or 466.9° C.) So if extraterrestrial life does exist in our solar system, Mars is still the most likely place.

Since 1965, we've sent probes to explore Mars. The chart below shows some of these probes.

Mars' Probes

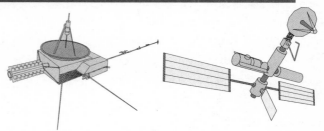

1965	*Mariner 4*
1969	*Mariner 6, 7* send pictures of south pole
1971-72	*Mariner 9* first to orbit Mars
1976	*Viking 1, 2* take soil tests
1993	Mars *Observer* probe lost
1997	*Pathfinder Sojourner* robot roves Mars' surface, sampling air, soil, rocks
1998	Photos of dust storms on Mars
2001	*Surveyor* probe studies Mars' climate
2003	*Mars Surveyor* to land and collect data
2005	*ISRU Miser* probe to bring Mars' soil to Earth
2009-2015	Human mission to Mars planned, a three-year trip

Recently, there has been exciting news. Both the Hubble Space Telescope (placed in orbit in 1990) and the Surveyor probe found evidence that liquid water may exist just under the surface of Mars. If this is so, it may mean that primitive life once existed on Mars. There is no proof yet, but the search continues.

  NOTICE: Photocopying any part of this book is forbidden by law.

9   What is *extraterrestrial* life?

A   life on Earth

B   the simplest form of life

C   life in water

D   life on planets other than Earth

10   How are Mars and Earth different?

F   The atmosphere is thicker on Mars.

G   The atmosphere is thinner on Mars.

H   Earth is usually colder than Mars.

J   There is more water on Mars.

11   Life on Mars is unlikely. Which of the following details does NOT support this statement?

A   the temperature extremes

B   lack of water

C   harmful radiation

D   dust storms

Go On

NOTICE: Photocopying any part of this book is forbidden by law.

215

12   This selection is mostly about

    F   the conditions on Mars

    G   life in our solar system

    H   what Mars' atmosphere is like

    J   the Hubble Space Telescope

13   According to the information in the selection, which fact is caused by Mars' having a thin atmosphere?

    A   Radiation is weaker on Mars.

    B   Temperatures change quickly on Mars.

    C   Mars is farther from the sun than Earth is.

    D   Mars' orbit is shaped like an ellipse.

14   According to the chart, when is a human mission to Mars planned? Write your answer in a complete sentence.

_____

_____

NOTICE: Photocopying any part of this book is forbidden by law.

15 Think about what the selection told you about conditions on Mars, and imagine that humans are about to land there. Describe three conditions they would have to be prepared for, and what problems these conditions might cause. Use information from the article.

_____

_____

_____

_____

_____

_____

_____

_____

_____

_____

_____

_____

_____

_____

_____

_____

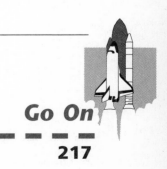

Go On

NOTICE: Photocopying any part of this book is forbidden by law.

16 Space exploration is very expensive. If humans are sent on a mission to Mars, there is a chance they may die. Considering the expense and the danger, do you think that we should continue to explore Mars? Give reasons for your response.

_____

_____

_____

_____

_____

_____

_____

_____

NOTICE: Photocopying any part of this book is forbidden by law.

Directions

Many great discoveries have been made by accident. Could a teen just be lucky? Read the selection. Then answer Numbers 17 through 25.

With a name like Kelly it's natural to love green. After all, I may be the first person born on the red planet, but my parents are Irish, and they do love green! Of course, my friends call me Careless Kelly, but maybe it'll be Lucky Kelly from now on.

I live in Alpha Base, the first Mars colony, built in 2028, just three years before I was born. My parents were original settlers. Mom's a chemist, and Dad is a geologist working on the search for underground water. Alpha Base was built two hundred meters beneath the surface of Mars, in the crater of an inactive volcano. The rim of the crater protects Alpha Base's entrance from dust storms.

You see, no one can live on the surface of Mars, at least not yet. There's been no proof that anything ever did. Mars is a frigid desert. And because Mars has practically no atmosphere, the sun's rays are deadly. You can't breathe the atmosphere, either. It's mostly carbon dioxide, the gas humans breathe out.

So, we live underground. There's no surface water. To produce water, we use machines to break down minerals in the rock; and we convert carbon dioxide into oxygen to breathe. Dad's team hopes some-day to find the water that scientists believe is trapped underground. I collect rocks, so he often brings me small samples when they drill down to a new level.

Go On

NOTICE: Photocopying any part of this book is forbidden by law.

219

Water is really precious here. I had to get special permission to use a liter of water for my school science project. So it was careless of me not to recycle the half liter I had left. Then, I accidentally dropped the new rock sample from Dad into the water. I was too busy with my experiment to fish it out. Leaving the Earthlight on in my workroom for two days was careless, too. It takes months to get new lightbulbs from Earth.

But if I hadn't done all those things, we wouldn't have proof. For millions of years, the proof must have been there, on the tiny piece of rock Dad brought me. When I put the rock in the water and exposed it to the Earthlight, the algae grew. Glorious one-celled green algae turned the water the most beautiful color in any world. Here was proof at last that primitive life once existed on Mars!

Oh, by the way –the scientists are going to name it for me—*Alga kelly*!

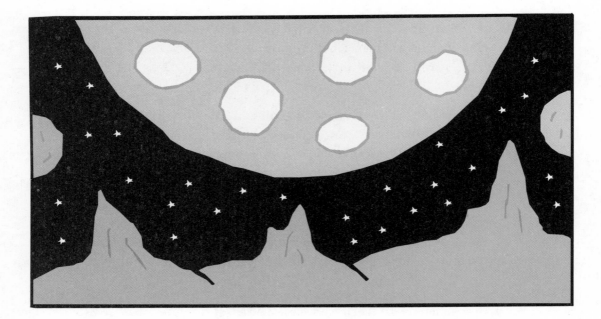

 NOTICE: Photocopying any part of this book is forbidden by law.

17   **The narrator in this story discovered**

A   underground water

B   proof of life on Mars

C   a special rock sample

D   a type of Earthlight

18   **Which of these events happened last?**

F   Kelly's Dad gave her a rock sample.

G   Kelly left the Earthlight on for two days.

H   Kelly dropped the rock sample into water.

J   Kelly got permission to use water for her science project.

19   **The narrator of this selection is**

A   a teenager living on Mars

B   an astronaut on the space station

C   a science student on Earth

D   a chemist living on Mars

Go On

NOTICE: Photocopying any part of this book is forbidden by law.

20 **"Call Me Lucky Kelly" is an example of**

F historical fiction

G science fiction

H nonfiction

J biography

21 **Think about "Call Me Lucky Kelly" and "Could There Be Life on Mars?" How are the selections alike?**

A Both are nonfiction.

B Both give information about Mars.

C Both are science fiction.

D Both take place in the future.

22 **Which statement best expresses the theme of "Call Me Lucky Kelly"?**

F Hard work pays off.

G You should not be careless.

H Water is the most precious thing.

J Some things happen by luck.

NOTICE: Photocopying any part of this book is forbidden by law.

23 You have read two selections that contain information about conditions on Mars. This chart shows the information each selection gives. There are three blank spaces in the chart. Fill in the missing information for each selection.

	Could There Be Life on Mars?	Call Me Lucky Kelly
water		no surface water; scientists searching for water underground
conditions on surface	usually very cold; very changeable, with extremes of temperature; dust storms	
atmosphere	thin; lets harmful radiation through; mostly carbon dioxide	

Go On

NOTICE: Photocopying any part of this book is forbidden by law.

223

24   Discuss some of the challenges the Mars settlers in the story faced. Use details from the story to support your answer.

In your answer, be sure to include

- the challenges involved in settling on Mars
- details from the story to support your answer

_____

_____

_____

_____

_____

_____

_____

_____

_____

_____

_____

_____

_____

_____

NOTICE: Photocopying any part of this book is forbidden by law.

25   Both "Could There Be Life on Mars?" and "Call Me Lucky Kelly" present information about the planet Mars. Suppose that you were asked to write a short report on the possibility of life on Mars. Explain which selection would be better to use, and why. In your answer, include a brief statement about the author's purpose for writing each selection.

_____

_____

_____

_____

_____

_____

_____

_____

_____

_____

Go On

NOTICE: Photocopying any part of this book is forbidden by law.

225

Directions

Read this story about traveling to the future. Then answer Numbers 26 through 33.

TRIP to TOMORROW

Wilson was always in high spirits, always the one for adventures. The minute he saw the ad for travel to the future, he signed up.

"That's for me!" he laughed. "This will be a blast!"

He bought two of the latest cameras and a very expensive tape recorder. When everything was ready, we sat in the family room to send him off on his great adventure.

"Have a wonderful trip," I said as I lifted my glass in a toast. "Don't stay in the future too long."

"I'll be back soon." Wilson grinned excitedly. "I promise."

I would have been scared and nervous. My friend was cheerful and excited, but then that was normal for Wilson.

It was time. Suddenly he started to shimmer and flicker.

He disappeared for what seemed only a second. Then he was back.

The return trip was perfectly timed. He didn't seem a moment older and he didn't look at all changed. I was shocked that the trip seemed to have happened in the blink of an eye. I had expected him to be away for several years.

"Well? How was it?" I asked excitedly.

"Well, I..." Wilson hesitated. He looked off into the distance and didn't finish the thought.

The silence grew longer. Then Wilson sighed. He shook his head. "I–I can't remember anything," he said at last.

"What do you mean you can't remember anything?" I wanted to shake him.

"Just that," he answered quietly. "I can't remember anything about what I saw in the future."

NOTICE: Photocopying any part of this book is forbidden by law.

"But what about the cameras and the tape recorder? You must have plenty on film and tape!"

Wilson sat quietly while I quickly checked the equipment. The film was blank. The tape was empty.

"Why?" I gasped. "Why didn't you record anything? Didn't the equipment work? Can't you remember *anything* at all?"

Wilson looked off into the distance. At last he spoke. "Well, I do remember one thing." Was his voice just a trifle sad?

"What? Tell me!" I hardly dared breathe.

"I do remember now... I was shown... things... in Earth's future. But then I was given a choice."

"What choice?" I asked anxiously.

"The choice of remembering it or not when I got back." Again he stared off quietly into the distance.

I shook my head. "And you chose to forget? But why? That's such a strange thing to do."

He turned to look at me. His eyes had a sad, haunted look.

"Isn't it?" he agreed. "I can't help wondering why."

Go On

NOTICE: Photocopying any part of this book is forbidden by law.

227

26 **Wilson doesn't remember anything about the future because**

 F he didn't really go to the future

 G he has lost his memory in an accident

 H he wants to keep his trip a secret

 J he chooses not to remember what he saw

27 **What does *in the blink of an eye* mean in this story?**

 A Wilson seems to have been gone for only a very brief time.

 B The speaker can't believe his eyes.

 C Wilson has to blink an eye to return from the future.

 D The speaker has to blink in order to get Wilson back.

28 **Which of the following statements is true?**

 F Before his trip, Wilson was usually sad and serious.

 G Wilson looks much older when he returns.

 H Wilson is excited and happy when he returns.

 J Wilson is changed by his trip.

29 **Reread this sentence from the story:**

"I do remember now... I was shown... things... in Earth's future."

Which sentence best explains the dots between words?

 A They show that Wilson is telling, not asking.

 B They show that Wilson is hesitating as he speaks.

 C They do not mean anything.

 D They mean the printer has extra ink.

NOTICE: Photocopying any part of this book is forbidden by law.

30 Choose the sentence that best explains the story's ending.

F Wilson saw something terrible in the future.

G In the future, life on Earth is wonderful.

H Wilson does not want to share his experience.

J In the future, cameras and tape recorders are useless.

31 A student wrote this dialog in a story. She made five mistakes in grammar, capitalization, and punctuation. Draw a line through each mistake and write the correction above it.

"Caitlin, this letter came for you today," said Mom.

Caitlin took the envelope. "I hope that's my answer," she said and ripped it open she scanned the letter's contents as her mother looked on curiously.

"I noticed its from the Hanson science Museum," said Mom. "What's this about?"

"Great news!" yelled Caitlin. "I've been accepted to the summer program. I can go, can't I, Mom"?

Her mother's smile was all she need for an answer.

Go On

NOTICE: Photocopying any part of this book is forbidden by law.

32 In this story, Wilson travels to the future and has a strange experience. Tell whether you think the experience changed Wilson, and how you know. Use details from the story that gave you clues to any changes.

In your answer, be sure to include

• whether you think Wilson was changed and, if so, how he was changed
• details from the story to support your answer

_____

_____

_____

_____

_____

_____

_____

_____

_____

_____

_____

_____

_____

_____

NOTICE: Photocopying any part of this book is forbidden by law.

33 The character in this story traveled to the future. If you were given the chance, would you want to see the future? Think about what you might learn and what the consequences might be. Explain your choice and support your answer.

_____

_____

_____

_____

_____

_____

_____

_____

Go On

NOTICE: Photocopying any part of this book is forbidden by law.

231

Directions

Have you ever wondered what astronauts eat in space? Read "Out-of-This-World Food" and find out. Then answer Numbers 34 through 41.

OUT-OF-THIS-WORLD FOOD

On April 12, 1961, Russian astronaut Yuri Gagarin became the first human in space. His trip was very short—only 108 minutes. It's a good thing he didn't stay any longer, because he might have been hungry. Since no one knew whether people could swallow food in the weightlessness of space, Gagarin didn't pack food. It's just as well: the food would have been hard to eat and it would have tasted terrible.

The early astronauts had to put up with freeze-dried powders and mush stuffed into aluminum tubes. John Glenn was America's first astronaut to eat in space. He found it was easy enough, but he did not like the mush in a tube. When he got back to Earth, one of the first things Glenn asked for was a sandwich!

Early space food had everything that Glenn and the other *Mercury* astronauts needed to stay healthy. Unfortunately, it didn't taste good.

The astronauts complained, and the food improved somewhat. The first things to go were the squeeze tubes. Instead, bite-sized cubes of food were coated with gelatin, a substance like jelly, to keep them from crumbling. After all, who wants lots of crumbs floating around the space capsule? The freeze-dried foods were placed in a special plastic container to make adding water easier, too.

Better packaging also meant better food quality and improved menus. The *Gemini* astronauts (1965–1966) had the choice of such foods as shrimp cocktail, chicken and vegetables, butterscotch pudding, and apple-sauce. They could select meal combinations themselves, too.

By the time of the *Apollo* program (1967–1972), the astronauts had hot water. This made preparing foods easier and improved the food's taste, too. The *Apollo* astronauts were also the first to use a "spoon bowl," a plastic container of food. The contents could be eaten with a spoon. The high moisture content of the food kept it stuck to the spoon so it didn't go floating around the cabin!

On *Skylab* (mid-1970s), the astronauts had more room, so they had a real dining room and table. They had footholds so they

 NOTICE: Photocopying any part of this book is forbidden by law.

could sit while they ate. They had the usual knife, fork, and spoon, and one more utensil—a pair of scissors to cut open plastic seals. And by now, the menu had grown to include seventy-two different food items.

On the present Space Shuttle, food is prepared in a galley, or kitchen, which contains a water dispenser and an oven. The astronauts use meal trays attached to their laps. The tray keeps the foods from floating away, so the astronauts don't have to finish one food before opening another. The astronauts even get to choose their own menus.

On the International Space Station, the Shuttle stops by with deliveries of fresh fruits and vegetables, but they only last a few days. Most of the time the astronauts rely on the pre-packaged space rations.

The astronauts would love to have more fresh foods. So why not have them grow fresh fruits and vegetables in space? For years, NASA has been working on ways to do just that.

There are lots of details to be worked out. For example, finding just the right plant varieties for the "space garden" is a painstaking process. The ideal space-plant would have short stalks to save room, would grow well in low light, and would be resistant to diseases. It would grow quickly, too.

Scientists are developing just these kinds of plants. So, some day the astronauts may sit down to a fresh salad of space-grown tomatoes and lettuce. That's a far cry from mush in a tube!

Go On

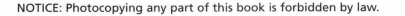

NOTICE: Photocopying any part of this book is forbidden by law.

34 **Which statement below is true?**

F John Glenn was the first man in space.

G The first foods the astronauts ate were delicious.

H John Glenn ate a sandwich in space.

J The first space foods were hard to eat and tasted terrible.

35 **A *utensil* is**

A a type of vegetable

B a machine aboard the Space Shuttle

C a tool used in the kitchen, especially to eat

D a type of food dispenser

36 **Here is a timeline that shows part of the history of food in space.**

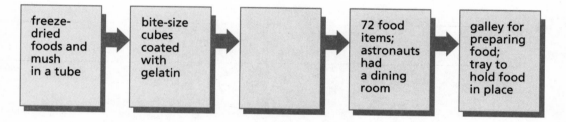

What belongs in the empty box?

F space-grown salads

G hot water and a "spoon bowl"

H fresh fruits and vegetables

J food in aluminum tubes

37 **One of the problems with preparing food in space is**

A it is very difficult to swallow

B things float around the cabin

C no one has time to eat

D all foods taste terrible

NOTICE: Photocopying any part of this book is forbidden by law.

38 **The author probably wrote this article**

F   to make people buy space foods

G   to give information about space food

H   to make people want to grow fresh food

J   to make people want to eat mush

39 **The sentences below contain four mistakes in capitalization, grammar, and punctuation. Rewrite the sentences correctly on the lines below.**

The apollo astronauts was the first to use spoons to eat in space. Having hot water made preparing their meals more easier too.

_____

_____

_____

_____

Go On

NOTICE: Photocopying any part of this book is forbidden by law.

235

40 The selection you have read gives a lot of information about the history of food in space. Summarize the main points of the article.

In your answer, be sure to include

- information about each group of astronauts: *Mercury*, *Gemini*, *Apollo*, *Skylab*, and Space Shuttle
- details from the selection to support your answer

_____

_____

_____

_____

_____

_____

_____

_____

_____

_____

_____

_____

_____

_____

NOTICE: Photocopying any part of this book is forbidden by law.

41 NASA scientists have spent a lot of time and effort improving food in space. They are also developing plants that can be grown in space. Do you think this work is important? "After all," some people say, "as long as the astronauts' food has all the vitamins, minerals, and calories they need, why does it matter?" Decide whether you think the improvements you read about are important. Write your opinion and give reasons to support your answer.

_____

_____

_____

_____

_____

_____

_____

Go On

NOTICE: Photocopying any part of this book is forbidden by law.

Directions

The International Space Station is our latest space project. What is it all about? Read the selection and then answer Numbers 42 through 49.

BUILDING the Space Station

Two-hundred-fifty miles above the Earth is a floating laboratory—the International Space Station. The ISS consists of several modules, or parts, including living quarters, a docking station, and laboratories. It won't be finished until 2006. Those in favor of it say that besides being a high-tech lab, it will be a launching pad for missions to Mars and beyond. But critics say it isn't worth the cost.

The idea for the space station was first proposed in 1984 by President Ronald Reagan. Back then, it would have cost $8 billion and was to be ready by 1992. Nothing came of the plans. Then in 1993, President Clinton revived the idea and made it a joint project with Russia. Some experts say it will cost close to $100 billion at completion.

Russia is supposed to pay a good portion of that, but Russia has been having money problems at home. To raise money, Russia has sold advertising. One booster rocket carried a huge logo advertising a fast food restaurant!

In April 2001, although NASA objected, the Russians allowed Dennis Tito, an American millionaire, to visit the station. The $20 million he paid was enough to pay their share of the flight.

Many Partners

The U.S. is developing the major portion of the space station. It will also build and pay for major systems such as temperature control, life support, the ground operations and communications systems. Russia is providing two research modules and early living quarters called the Service Module. Russia has also built a solar power platform and supplies the *Soyuz* spacecraft for crew return and transfer. In addition to Russia, fourteen other countries are involved in the project.

Japan is contributing a laboratory module. Canada is contributing a 55-foot robotic arm that will help move equipment in space. Italy and Brazil, as well as ten European countries, will all take part in the project.

NOTICE: Photocopying any part of this book is forbidden by law.

Why Spend the Money?

The sixteen countries building the space station believe the benefits will one day outweigh the risks and the enormous expense. NASA believes the most important benefit is that the space station allows humans to live and work for long periods in the "weightless" environment of space. The space station gives scientists a unique chance to study how the human body and other things behave in a world without gravity. Everything in our bodies, from our heartbeat to the thickness of our bones, is affected by gravity.

Chemicals behave differently without gravity, too. This means that materials could be combined and new substances created that are impossible to produce on Earth. Scientists hope these experiments will lead to new treatments for cancer, AIDS, and other serious diseases.

Other experiments will examine processes like burning. The information from these experiments may help scientists design cars and factories that burn energy more cleanly.

"It's going to take time to get the ISS constructed and functional," said John Charles, a NASA scientist. "But when it's finished, we're going to be amazed by what we learn—and we're going to wonder how we did without it for so long."

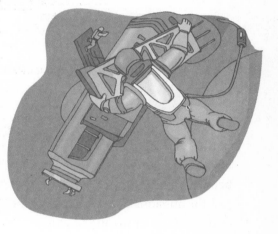

42　**The International Space Station is**

F　complete now

G　located in Russia

H　due to be completed in 2006

j　sponsored mostly by Canada

43　**What does critic mean in this article?**

A　a type of scientist

B　a person who writes a review of a play or book

C　a person who wants to build the space station

D　someone who finds fault with something

44　**What is the best clue that this passage is nonfiction?**

F　The author tells what low gravity does.

G　The passage has facts and figures.

H　The subject is interesting.

J　The passage contains a quote from a scientist.

Go On

NOTICE: Photocopying any part of this book is forbidden by law.

45 Which sentence in paragraph 7 best states the main idea of that paragraph?

A Sixteen countries are involved in building the space station.

B The earth's gravity influences many things.

C On the space station, scientists can study how things behave in a world without gravity.

D Our bones are affected by gravity.

46 What is the author's main purpose in writing the section under the heading "Why Spend the Money?"

F to state reasons against building the space station

G to get the readers' attention

H to explain what scientists hope to learn from the space station

J to sell advertising on the space station

47 Each country on the chart below has made contributions to the space station. Use the information in the article to fill in the missing information in the chart.

Country	Contribution(s)
	temperature control and life support systems; ground operations and communications systems
	research modules; solar power platform; *Soyuz* spacecraft
Canada	
Japan	laboratory module

NOTICE: Photocopying any part of this book is forbidden by law.

48 Suppose you are a scientist working aboard the space station. What would you say in response to someone who thinks building the space station is a waste of time and money? Use details from the selection to support your answer.

_____

_____

_____

_____

_____

_____

_____

_____

_____

_____

_____

_____

_____

_____

_____

Go On

NOTICE: Photocopying any part of this book is forbidden by law.

49 Russia has tried to raise money to fund its part in the space station by selling advertising and by accepting tourists as visitors to the station. So far the U.S. has disapproved of having non-professionals (tourists) in space. Do you agree or disagree? Present your argument and support it with reasons.

_____

_____

_____

_____

_____

_____

_____

_____

NOTICE: Photocopying any part of this book is forbidden by law.

Directions

Read this selection about the two largest planets. Then answer Numbers 50 through 58.

GAS GIANTS

Astronauts may reach Mars early this century. But even if it were not for the great distances, it is unlikely that anyone will ever land on Jupiter or Saturn. Why not? There's nothing solid to land on.

Jupiter and Saturn (along with Uranus and Neptune) are known as the gas giants. Unlike Mercury, Venus, Earth, and Mars, which are composed mostly of rock and metals, and have solid surfaces, the "gas giants" are composed of—well, gas.

Jupiter is mostly hydrogen and helium, with small amounts of methane, ammonia, and water vapor. The atmosphere of Jupiter is very deep, and the gas simply gets denser with depth. The center of Jupiter is a very hot rocky core, and the planet radiates heat. It actually gives off more energy in heat than it gets from the sun.

What we see when we look at Jupiter through a telescope is the top of the atmosphere. Jupiter is a place of violent storms. High winds blow across the planet, arranging the clouds into wide, colorful bands. A huge storm center (twice the size of Earth) known as the "red spot" has existed for at least three hundred years. The winds of this permanent storm swirl counter-clockwise at speeds of 400 miles per hour.

Jupiter is named for Jove, the king of the gods in Greek mythology. It is well-named, for Jupiter is truly huge, the largest of the planets. If Jupiter were a hollow ball, more than a thousand Earths could fit inside.

Jupiter is bright, too—the fourth brightest object in the sky. It has been known since early times. The astronomer Galileo studied it by telescope in 1610 and discovered four of Jupiter's sixteen moons.

When Voyager 1 visited Jupiter in 1979, scientists got a wonderful surprise. The cameras showed that like Saturn, Jupiter has rings! Jupiter's rings are fainter and smaller and probably composed of rock.

Go On

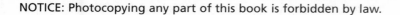

NOTICE: Photocopying any part of this book is forbidden by law.

The latest spacecraft to visit Jupiter is *Galileo*, launched in 1989. It is orbiting Jupiter now and continues to send back photos.

Saturn is the sixth planet from the sun and the second largest. It has at least eighteen moons. Like Jupiter, it has been known since prehistoric times and was first seen through a telescope by Galileo. The astronomer Huygens noted the rings in 1659. It was thought that Saturn was unique in having rings until Voyager 1 proved otherwise. We now know Uranus and Neptune have them, too.

Like Jupiter, Saturn consists of many layers of gases—mostly hydrogen and helium. The top layer appears as "bands" of clouds, much fainter than Jupiter's. At Saturn's center is liquid hydrogen around a rocky inner core. Saturn also has a red storm spot. And like Jupiter, Saturn's center is hot, and although scientists aren't sure why, Saturn seems to glow faintly from within.

While Jupiter's rings are dark and narrow, Saturn's rings are wide, bright and beautiful. The rings look solid from Earth, but they actually consist of millions of small particles each in its own orbit. The particles are ice crystals, or rock covered with ice. They range in size from a centimeter or so to several meters. Saturn's rings are also extremely thin.

There is still much we don't know about the gas giants. For instance, what is the origin of the rings? Why are Jupiter's rings dark, while Saturn's are bright? Why do the "red spots" on both planets persist? The Cassini spacecraft, launched in 1997, will reach orbit around Saturn in July 2004. Perhaps some of the mysteries of the gas planets will be solved then.

50 **There are not likely to be any manned missions to Saturn or Jupiter because**

   F   there is nothing solid to land on

   G   these planets have rings

   H   these planets are too large

   J   these planets are solid rock

NOTICE: Photocopying any part of this book is forbidden by law.

51 **To say that people thought Saturn was *unique* means**

A   it was wide and flat

B   it was glowing

C   it was one of a kind

D   it was ordinary

52 **One difference between Saturn and Jupiter is**

F   Jupiter is mostly hydrogen and Saturn is mostly helium

G   Saturn was discovered by Galileo

H   Saturn has rings

J   Jupiter is much larger than Saturn

53 **The Cassini spacecraft will probably**

A   crash into Jupiter

B   take photos of Saturn

C   land on Saturn

D   land on Jupiter

54 **Where else would you be most likely to find an article like this?**

F   in a short-story anthology

G   on the editorial page of a newspaper

H   in a science textbook

J   in a magazine of popular culture

Go On

55 If you wanted to find out the very latest information about Jupiter or Mars, which of these resources would be most helpful?

   A a novel

   B an encyclopedia

   C an atlas

   D the Internet

56 Look at the diagram. Some of the information about Jupiter and Saturn is filled in for you. Find three facts in the article that show things Jupiter and Saturn have in common. Fill in the empty lines.

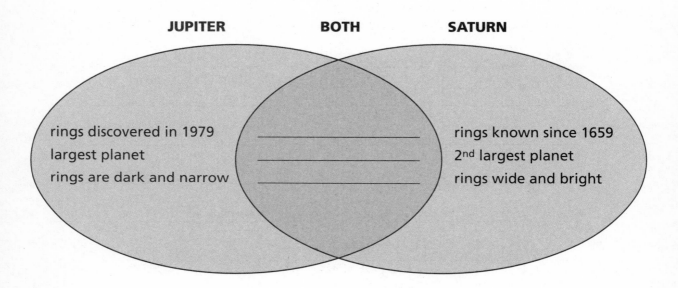

JUPITER   **BOTH**   **SATURN**

rings discovered in 1979   _____   rings known since 1659
largest planet   _____   2nd largest planet
rings are dark and narrow   _____   rings wide and bright

NOTICE: Photocopying any part of this book is forbidden by law.

57 The article gives you much information about Jupiter and Saturn. Write two paragraphs which sum up the information known about each planet. In your paragraphs, compare and contrast the two planets.

_____

_____

_____

_____

_____

_____

_____

_____

_____

_____

_____

_____

_____

_____

_____

Go On

NOTICE: Photocopying any part of this book is forbidden by law.

247

58 The article tells you that, besides Saturn and Jupiter, Neptune and Uranus are also gas planets. Based on the information the article provides about Jupiter and Saturn, what characteristics would you expect to find on Neptune and Uranus?

_____

_____

_____

_____

_____

_____

_____

_____

 NOTICE: Photocopying any part of this book is forbidden by law.

Directions

From 1957 to the late 1960s, the U.S. and the Soviet Union raced each other to prove superiority in space. Read about the space race. Then answer Numbers 59 through 68.

THE RACE TO THE MOON

In 1957, an aluminum ball only 23 inches in diameter stunned the world. It was *Sputnik*, the first artificial satellite, and it was launched into orbit around the Earth by the Soviet Union. The world was changed forever.

Since the end of World War II (1939–1945), the world's two strongest countries, the United States and the Soviet Union, had been rivals in a struggle known as the Cold War. Both knew the other was developing long-range missiles that could carry bombs, and each lived in fear of the other starting a war. The United States thought its technology was far ahead of that of the Soviet Union— until *Sputnik*.

The idea that the Soviet Union had the ability to put a satellite into orbit above the Earth frightened many Americans. Were we falling behind in the technology race? The U.S. rushed to catch up. Congress quickly passed a bill called the National Defense Education Act, giving schools more money for math and science programs.

Next, in 1958, the government set up the National Aeronautics and Space Administration (NASA) to organize the space program. By the end of that year, the U.S. had successfully launched three satellites to gather information about the Earth's atmosphere.

But the Soviet Union was still ahead. One month after *Sputnik*, it launched *Sputnik* 2, putting a dog named Laika into orbit. In 1959 Russia sent a probe to land on the moon. In April 1961, Yuri Gagarin became the first human to orbit Earth.

In May 1961, the U.S. finally sent an astronaut (Alan Shepard) into space for fifteen minutes. But he did not orbit the Earth, and the U.S. was clearly still behind in the race.

Go On

NOTICE: Photocopying any part of this book is forbidden by law.

249

Yet, so far, no one was really sure of what would count as *winning* the race. It was President John F. Kennedy who set the goal for the U.S. in a speech to Congress in 1961. He called for the United States to put a man on the moon by the end of the 1960s. "No single space project will be more important to mankind or more important in the long-range exploration of space," Kennedy said.

Americans were inspired. Suddenly everyone—the government, the military, the scientific community, and private industry— all began to work together. More than 400,000 people were involved. Nothing like this had ever happened outside of wartime.

Slowly the U.S. began to catch up. In 1962, John Glenn became the first American to orbit Earth. In 1965, Edward White became the first American to walk in space. Next, the U.S. sent several unpiloted spacecrafts into orbit around the moon. They took photos of the moon's surface to identify the best spot for a landing. On Christmas Eve 1968, Apollo 8 carried three astronauts into orbit around the moon.

Then, in July 1969, *Apollo 11* took off carrying astronauts Neil Armstrong, Edwin "Buzz" Aldrin, and Michael Collins. Three days later, the world watched on television while Armstrong and Aldin stepped out of the moon lander onto the surface of the moon. Through the static Armstrong said, "That's one small step for Man, one giant leap for mankind."

Today instead of rivalry, there is cooperation, as the United States, Russia, and fourteen other nations work together to design, build, and assemble the International Space Station that now orbits the Earth.

NOTICE: Photocopying any part of this book is forbidden by law.

59   The first artificial satellite was launched into space by

- **A**   President Kennedy
- **B**   the Soviet Union
- **C**   the United States
- **D**   the Cold War

60   The first human to go into space was

- **F**   Laika
- **G**   Yuri Gagarin
- **H**   Alan Shepard
- **J**   President Kennedy

61   Had the U.S. been the first country to launch a satellite into space instead of the Soviet Union, the Russians would have probably

- **A**   been happy and excited
- **B**   stayed out of the space race
- **C**   declared war on the U.S.
- **D**   increased their efforts to improve their space technology

62   Many Americans were frightened by the launch of Sputnik because

- **F**   it carried a nuclear bomb
- **G**   it showed the Soviet Union had superior technology
- **H**   it carried a spy camera
- **J**   it could fall at any time

Go On

NOTICE: Photocopying any part of this book is forbidden by law.

63 The American government, the military, the scientific community, and private industry all worked together to put a man on the moon. Which of the following is probably NOT a reason why they did this?

A They were inspired by President Kennedy's speech.

B They wanted to show that the U.S. was superior to the Soviet Union.

C They were hoping to get rich.

D Their pride in the United States was at stake.

64 Here is a timeline of some events in the space race.

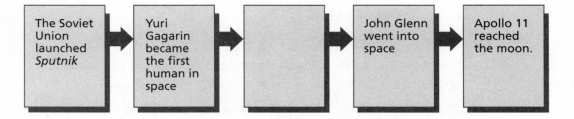

Which statement belongs in the empty box?

F Neil Armstrong walked on the moon.

G The Soviets put a dog into space.

H President Kennedy called for the U.S. to reach the moon.

J The Cold War began.

65 Which answer best explains the author's purpose in writing this piece?

A to give information about the history of the race to the moon

B to entertain with an adventure about space

C to persuade Americans to support the space program

D to convince people the space program is important

     NOTICE: Photocopying any part of this book is forbidden by law.

66   **The sentences below contain four mistakes in capitalization, punctuation and usage. Rewrite the sentences correctly on the lines below.**

The Soviet union it was the rival of the United States Both countries was worried that the other would start a nuclear war.

_____

_____

_____

_____

Go On

NOTICE: Photocopying any part of this book is forbidden by law.

67 Suppose that you were a young person living in the late 1950s or early
1960s. How do you think you would have felt during the time the U.S.
and the Soviet Union were racing each other to be first on the moon?
Include how you might have reacted as you learned about the advances
each country made. Support your answer with details from the selection.

_____

_____

_____

_____

_____

_____

_____

_____

_____

_____

_____

_____

_____

_____

_____

_____

 NOTICE: Photocopying any part of this book is forbidden by law.

68 Why do you think the United States and the Soviet Union each tried so hard to become the first to reach the moon? Think about reasons each might have had and back up your response with details from the article.

_____

_____

_____

_____

_____

_____

_____

_____

STOP

NOTICE: Photocopying any part of this book is forbidden by law.